Drink & Tell

Over 500 Cocktail Recipes Created in Boston

Frederic Yarm

Copyright

Table of Contents

"One cocktail is just like one revolution,
it just gets you organized for the next."

An adaptation of a Will Rogers quote.

Acknowledgements

First, I would like to thank everyone who helped out before there was even a concept of a book. This includes all of the bartenders in Boston who shared not only recipes but their love of the art. Also, Andrea Desrosiers for being my companion in the drink world, Jessica Marcus for starting the Cocktail Virgin blog and inviting me along, and DrinkBoston's Lauren Clark for words of encouragement along the way.

When I began collecting recipes and writing the blog, the original concept was not to write a book but to journal my cocktail experiences and to promote the bar programs across town and the creativity and hospitality of individual bartenders. A few people did ask if I was planning to do a book, but for the longest while, it was not a goal and it never amounted to more than me bandying about the idea for a few moments at a time. However, my job situation took a turn south a few months ago, and I had a bit of spare time on my hands. One day as I was fixing my friend's computer, his mom, a retired school teacher, chatted with me about my life and then declared that I need to write a book. So to Ed Walters' mom, thank you for motivating me. I am also thankful for the publishing-world guidance from Cecilia Tan, Ed Walters, and Stephanie Schorow who have helped with everything from software to marketing advice. I would also like to thank Luke O'Neil for his published notes on the history of the Boston cocktail scene which were incredibly helpful in organizing my thoughts. Moreover, thank you to Sahil Mehta, Mark Yarm, and Andrea Desrosiers for their time and efforts in editing this book.

While the photos on the front and back covers, like all the photos in the book, are mine, I would like to give a nod to Backbar's Joe Cammarata for preparing such a stunning Back Word for the front. And a special thanks to Molly Hopper and the rest of Eastern Standard for allowing me to alter their cocktail napkin for the back.

Dedicated to those merry souls
who make drinking a pleasure,
who achieve contentedness long
before capacity, and who,
whenever they drink, prove able
to carry it, enjoy it, and remain
ladies and gentlemen.

A Trader Vic quote that decorated one of the letterboards at Drink.

Introduction

Shortly after *Left Coast Libations* came out in 2010, a few people asked if I would consider doing a similar treatment for the right coast. I joked that the New York City aspect alone would fill up a book. Upon looking at all of the recipes that I have collected over the years through my work on the Cocktail Virgin blog and before, I realized that Boston itself had more than enough material to fly solo. Besides, it is the city with which I am best acquainted. The cocktail scenes in New York, Philadelphia, D.C., and other right coast locations were ones that I learned about solely from short forays, published recipes, or second-hand knowledge. What I drank and what I made from recipes from these other cities I definitely enjoyed, but it still felt like another world.

While the cocktail recipes I have collected are by no means a reflection of the bar scene in Boston as a whole, my wanderings have taken me from hot bars and restaurants with renowned bar programs to small neighborhood places with hidden gems of talent. From fancy to dive, from high volume to low, these bars that I frequented all share a respect for the craft cocktail movement. With one foot firmly planted on the classics, the bartenders at these bars seem to take great joy in creating great modern retellings of our past.

One of the great aspects of the Boston drink scene is the collegial and noncompetitive air of the bartenders. The most obvious example for me is how open they are to relating recipes, explaining techniques, recommending other places to go, and the like. However, the more important form of communication is that which they share among each other. By sitting at one another's bars, they learn from each other – not just the shared recipes and techniques, but the overall culture that Boston has been fostering. Through this, the Boston cocktail scene has grown its own distinct identity.

In one sense, the rebirth of Boston craft bartending can be traced back to the now defunct B Side Lounge in Cambridge. Behind the stick there, many of our city's finest bartenders learned the art. Over time and with the aid of diasporas, other centers of higher drink learning and training popped up. In these second and third waves, places like Eastern Standard, No. 9 Park, Drink, Craigie on Main, Green Street, and other bars began to take over the role.

As *Left Coast Libations* stresses, only visiting the establishments can give a good sense of what it is like to sit at the bar and interact with the cast of characters behind the stick. However, with this collection you can at least make the recipes and understand Boston's cocktail culture one potation at a time. And if you have experienced these bars firsthand, hopefully the recipes inside will be of some of your favorite drinks and will bring back fond memories. True, you can make each bar's drinks, but this does not steal from each establishment's glory – the bars are much more than an old set of recipes. Not only are they constantly evolving new recipes, many of these places have such a sense of hospitality that the drinks themselves are just the bonus. For example, knowing how Eastern Standard makes its Metamorphosis or Whiskey Smash does not diminish the number of times I go and visit, even though I can make those at home almost as well.

In compiling the book, I was inspired by the philosophies of *Beta Cocktails* in terms of how the majority of their recipes are easy to make. Likewise, I tried to eliminate from the collection all infusions, rare spirits, and house bitters that had no easy substitutes. Moreover, all of the syrups can either be commercially sourced or be made rather easily and quickly; even if kitchen work is outside of your realm, there are plenty of recipes inside that require no time at the stove. Granted, not every home bar has all of these reagents, nor can every budget or cramped living space support this list of ingredients; however, I hope that some of these recipes guide your purchases so you can intelligently round out your home collections and use your resources wisely.

The recipes that follow were all created in the last few years here in Boston and neighboring Cambridge and Somerville; in addition, I included a handful from Worcester, since some of the bartenders there also do shifts in Boston. Well, there are probably some misattributions, and I apologize in advance; hazy is the history that is retold like this, and lapses in communication do occur. The recipes are often presented as they were made for me, although some were adapted to make them more home bartender-friendly. Furthermore, a handful of recipes were sourced from various magazines, websites, and books, tested at home, and included in here as part of the city's tapestry. In addition, do not feel obligated to match the brands listed; use your best judgment to determine which spirit would match the flavor profile. Often, individual drink recipes were made with a variety of brands over the years, depending on what was on hand at the bar.

7

I did not include classics in the collection unless it was a Boston-made variation, as this book is meant to be a supplement to a basic library. I felt there was no need to recreate the wheel or take up space with recipes that have been published many times elsewhere. For those, I would recommend Robert Hess' *The Essential Bartender's Guide*, Dale DeGroff's *The Craft of the Cocktail*, and Gary Regan's *The Joy of Mixology* which all do it with panache.

In addition, this book was not meant to be a beginner's guide with an extensive section on technique. I would highly recommend learning the basics from the masters in the three books listed above. Another great way to learn is by taking classes offered in your town. The Boston Shaker store, for example, provides classes on basic technique, the role of bitters, and spirits tastings. Moreover, much can be gleaned online; I recommend watching Robert Hess' excellent *The Cocktail Spirit* video series. I also cannot stress enough the need for the right basic tools including a shaker, mixing glass, Julep strainer, Hawthorne strainer, bar spoon, and channel knife or vegetable peeler. And most importantly: jiggers! While there are a handful of bartenders across town whom I trust to free-pour accurately, I never recommend it. Many of the best here in Boston use jiggers or OXO measuring cups to get the precision and reproducibility they desire.

When I was thinking about how to lay out the recipe section of the book, I began flipping through my cocktail book collection. I kept returning to the simple elegance of the 1937 *Café Royal Cocktail Book*. While many cocktail drinkers have not heard of the book, they probably have had recipes that first appeared there, such as the Twentieth Century and the Lion's Tail. One thing I can relate to is how the author, William Tarling, collected recipes from his contemporaries in England and promoted individual bartenders through attribution. Indeed, Tarling captured the essence of what was going on in the London cocktail scene in the 1930s by writing about the UK Bartenders Guild's creations. Once the parallels became apparent, I decided to make the cocktail section of this book a homage to that great collection of drinks.

The Players: A Neighborhood by Neighborhood Approach

One of the best ways of thinking about bars in Boston is by neighborhood, since this provides the most options in case one bar is too crowded or unexpectedly closed for the evening. Moreover, it allows for convenient bar-hopping without great expenditure of time or transportation costs. While there are plenty of bars serving drinks and beer in these neighborhoods, I focused on the ones that I frequent and that have impressed me with their cocktail programs. This collection is meant to be the highlights of my favorite places and not an all-encompassing list of establishments. Pardon any sins of omission.

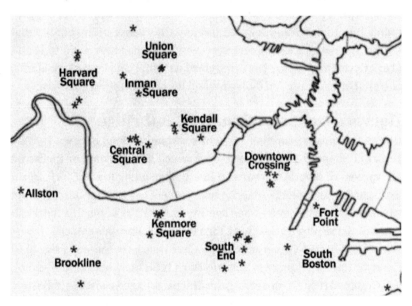

Central Square, Cambridge

Central Square is home to a growing community of craft cocktail bars. One of the longest-running programs there is **Green Street** (280 Green Street, Cambridge). Owner Dylan Black learned a lot of the trade at the B Side Lounge prior to opening Green Street, and once at Green Street, he worked with Misty Kalkofen and others to establish a large collection of classic cocktails and house originals. While the bartenders will often hand you a small cocktail menu, do not be afraid to ask for Green Street's large one, a six-sided A-to-Z affair. Nearby is **Rendezvous** (502 Massachusetts Avenue, Cambridge), where bar manager Scott Holliday shines with his old-world bartending charm. While more of a dining establishment, the drink program there is solid thanks to Scott's training at Chez Henri uptown. On the opposite side of the street is the newest spot in the area, **Brick and Mortar** (569 Massachusetts Avenue, Cambridge). The old B Side Lounge owner Patrick Sullivan reunited with his prodigy Misty Kalkofen to take over the space left vacant by the Enormous Room. In between Misty's time at the B Side Lounge and Brick and Mortar, she sharpened her cocktail-making skills at Green Street and Drink, and she has assembled an edgy cocktail program in a low-key atmosphere. Down the block is **Craigie on Main** (853 Main Street, Cambridge) which hosts a bar and lounge that are set off from the main dining room. When owner Tony Maws moved his restaurant from Craigie Street near Harvard Square, he hired Eastern Standard's Tom Schlesinger-Guidelli to set up the bar program. Tom took with him Eastern Standard's sense of hospitality and craft-drink making ideals, and even though he has moved on to Island Creek Oyster Bar, the bar has maintained its initial high level of standards; current bar manager Ted Gallagher and his crew continue to impress.

Harvard to Porter Square, Cambridge

One of the longest-running existent cocktail bastions in town is **Chez Henri** (1 Shepard Street, Cambridge) which has spawned or furthered the careers of several top barmen in town including Joe McGuirk, Dylan Black, and Scott Holliday, despite being one of the smaller bars. Current bar manager Rob Kraemer has continued the level of quality. A certain cocktail sleuth also tracked back the Periodista, Boston's cult classic version of an obscure Cuban cocktail, to Chez Henri. On the way from Chez Henri to Harvard Square is **Temple Bar** (1688 Massachusetts Avenue), which gained respect for serving the first barrel-aged cocktails in Boston. The bar program there prospered when they gained bar manager Alex Homans from sister establishment Russell House Tavern. And speaking of that establishment, **Russell House Tavern** (14 John F. Kennedy Street, Cambridge) got off to a good start when they acquired Drink alum Aaron Butler to start up their cocktail program. Sporting a bar on each of the two levels, the cocktail program showcases a solid collection of classic and original drinks. Newest in Harvard Square is **Park Restaurant** (59 John F. Kennedy Street, Cambridge) which delivers well-executed cocktails ranging from pleasing to challenging.

Kendall Square, Cambridge

Kendall Square has a growing number of cocktail bars with the oldest one, **Hungry Mother** (233 Cardinal Medeiros Avenue, Cambridge), having only opened a few years ago. The drinks at Hungry Mother have an unique aesthetic since the bar program was founded by bartenders with less formal training and more of a sense of what works well in the glass. Up until recently, the drinks were numbered which seemed odd until you gained a certain affection to a #43 or #65. On the other side of the square is **Abigail's** (291 3rd Street, Cambridge) with its stunning bar made from a cross section of a tree. Headed by B Side Lounge and Chez Henri alum Rob Iurilli, the bar program has produced some interesting drinks. Finally, the newest edition is **West Bridge** (1 Kendall Square, Cambridge), whose bar program is headed by Eastern Standard alum Josh Taylor.

Inman Square, Camberville

Inman Square has a pair of cocktail bars on its outskirts that I adore. **Trina's Starlite Lounge** (3 Beacon Street, Somerville) is an eclectic mix of a neighborhood bar and restaurant and an industry hangout; similarly, their take on mixology ranges from lighthearted to classic. Furthermore, their Monday industry brunch is one of the best places to see your favorite bartenders on your side of the bar. Down the street from Trina's is **Bergamot** (118 Beacon Street, Somerville), an upscale restaurant with a bar. And behind that bar are Craigie on Main alums Paul Manzelli and Kai Gagnon, who not only mix great drinks (as you would expect from their pedigree) but make the bar extra hospitable with their entertaining personalities and showmanship especially once the diners have left.

Union Square, Somerville

The longest-running cocktail bar in Union Square is the **Independent** (75 Union Square, Somerville). The program was made notable by bar manager Evan Harrison before he went on to Deep Ellum and Brick and Mortar; in his wake is a bar program that is still going strong with high-quality cocktails and a doubled number of tap lines. The bar is actually a two-sided affair with one half being a lounge that frequently has local DJs playing music and the other half being the restaurant which has a more subdued vibe. Around the corner is the relative newcomer, **Backbar** (9 Sanborn Court, Somerville), which was launched by the Journeyman restaurant in the adjoining part of the old Ford Dealership building in which they reside. When they hired Drink alum Sam Treadway to head the bar program, they scored not only a knowledgeable and talented barman, but one with a cultish following. Despite the short menu, they have rotating drink-of-the-day and -week specials, as well as mental and physical drink libraries that they can tap into. While technically not in Union Square, **Highland Kitchen** (150 Highland Avenue, Somerville) is only a short walk away, and I grouped it here for it is not in a square proper but in a nearby residential area. Due to its location, it has a large following in the neighborhood. Though some of the drinks are more pleasing to the masses, the collection of bartenders there includes B Side Lounge and Green Street alumni as well as other talented drink makers who have put some more adventurous drink offerings on the menu.

Kenmore Square, Boston

In the middle of Kenmore Square is the hat trick of Hotel Commonwealth's establishments. The oldest of the three is **Eastern Standard** (528 Commonwealth Avenue, Boston), which lays claim to the longest marble bar in Boston. Under the tutelage of Jackson Cannon, the bar has generated some inventive cocktails as well as major players in the Boston cocktail scene. With a focus on hospitality, the bar is quite dynamic, especially if you catch the transition from a bar one deep with craft cocktail enthusiasts to a post-game Red Sox crowd four or more deep. Eastern Standard is also one of the popular industry hangouts, especially late at night as the kitchen stays open until 1:30 a.m. The next oldest of the trio is **Island Creek Oyster Bar** (500 Commonwealth Avenue, Boston), which seems to have the art of creating food-friendly cocktail lists down to a science. The drinks range from aperitifs to Tiki libations, all served with the same level of hospitality as Eastern Standard. The newest one is **Hawthorne** (500A Commonwealth Avenue, Boston), which is their upscale cocktail lounge. Jackson Cannon brought together a dream team of bartenders from across town as well as from Manhattan to execute drink making to perfection. While the bar seats provide a familiar feel, the couches and armchairs in the lounge make it seem as if you are at a friend's posh home for a cocktail party. On the other side of Fenway Park is the **Citizen Public House** (1310 Boylston Avenue, Boston) from the owners of the Franklin Café. Bar manager Joy Richard and her team offer a solid list of cocktails, Swizzles, and Juleps as a diversion from their immense whiskey list and Fernet Branca on tap. The fifth bar in the area, **Clio** (370 Commonwealth Avenue), is not technically in Kenmore Square but is in walking distance and not easily grouped with another cocktail nexus. Between bar manager

Todd Maul's excellent palate, respect for the classics, and tinkering with molecular mixology, the menu is a sizeable booklet filled with an impressive array of offerings. Todd's attention to detail, whether via a Tiki drink or a variation on a pre-Prohibition cocktail, brings the art of drink to another level.

Park Street & Downtown Crossing, Boston

One of the epicenters of the craft cocktail scene is hidden within the fine-dining establishment of **No. 9 Park** (9 Park Street, Boston). With a bar program that has been led by such greats as Drink's John Gertsen, it has maintained its high level of quality with current bar manager Ted Kilpatrick. With their success that started with the Palmyra, they have succeeded in making inventive drinks throughout the years for an eclectic crowd of loyal fans. A few blocks away from Park Street is Temple Place, home to two solid bars. The first is **Stoddard's Fine Food & Ale** (48 Temple Place, Boston) with its majestic dark wood bar that fills the historic space. Bar manager Jamie Walsh has assembled a talented crew of bartenders as well as a cocktail menu filled with classics listed by year and a few classics-inspired originals. Moreover, their tap-beer menu always has tempting offerings to momentarily lure me away from the cocktails. The second is **J.M. Curley** (21 Temple Place, Boston); although their program is rather new, they have all the hallmarks of a solid cocktail bar. Another Boston cocktail landmark is **Silvertone** (69 Bromfield Street) which is a low-key, subterranean establishment that serves as another of the city's industry hangouts.

South End & Back Bay, Boston

In Boston, there are two Franklins, and the one in the South End is the **Franklin Café** (278 Shawmut Avenue, Boston). Both share overlapping cocktail menus and are quite popular with the industry crowd for their late food and last-call hours. Moreover, bartenders from the owners' other restaurant, the Citizen Public House, often do shifts there. Nearby are **Aquitaine** (569 Tremont Street, Boston) and the **Beehive** (541 Tremont Street, Boston), which have pleased me with their cocktail offerings on the few times that I have been there. A few blocks away is **The Gallows** (1395 Washington Street, Boston) which sports an interesting menu thanks to the interplay between the kitchen, bartenders, and managers in creating drink concepts. Also of merit is a pair of restaurants that do amazing things with cordial licenses. The first is **Estragon** (700 Harrison

Avenue, Boston), which is a Spanish restaurant in the South End. It has some decent offerings on the cocktail menu, but the real strength of the program comes from the off-list creations of Sahil Mehta, who crafts some more challenging drinks using his superb palate. The other is **Coppa** (253 Shawmut Avenue, Boston), where the bar program was started by Courtney Bissonnette, a B Side Lounge and No. 9 Park alum. Between these two cordial license bars, it is easy to forget that they work with limitations on what spirits they can carry and serve; perhaps the limitations themselves push them to be more creative with their recipes, such as their respective beer cocktails. Courtney also worked on the bar program at **Toro** (1704 Washington Street, Boston), which has some fine cocktail offerings executed by B Side Lounge and Eastern Standard alumni. Of note is the Spanish restaurant's love of sherry, which appears in a few drinks including a Sherry Julep.

Allston & Brookline

In the midst of the music clubs and student bars in Allston is **Deep Ellum** (477 Cambridge Street, Allston). While the bar usually gets touted for its solid and eclectic beer program, bar manager Max Toste learned more than that from his time at Bukowski's. From house originals to Max's takes on classics, the cocktail program has garnered as much respect from imbibers across town as their beer program has. Next door is the **Lone Star Taco Bar** (477 Cambridge Street, Allston) owned by the same people as Deep Ellum. Although the bar program is less adventurous than Deep Ellum's, their collection of mezcal and tequila drinks are made with the same care and attention, often by bartenders who work at both establishments. Up Harvard Street into Brookline is **Lineage** (242 Harvard Street, Brookline), where the bar program took off with the help of then bar manager Ryan Lotz. Well before leaving to go to Hawthorne, Ryan trained Brendan Pratt to take over and continue the legacy of well thought-out and crafted cocktails. And even further up the road is **Pomodoro** (24 Harvard Street, Brookline), where on Mondays and a few other nights during the week, many industry folk seek out the wisdom and drinks of Stephen Shellenberger.

Fort Point & South Boston

In the midst of the old industrial center of Fort Point, John Gertsen from No. 9 Park built up **Drink** (348 Congress Street, Boston) in an old wool factory. Without a bar menu, drink orders turn into conversations about base spirits, flavors, and genres. The talented and creative bartenders integrate these ideas, set off to fetch bottles, and return with classics and original cocktails and Highballs. Another innovation in the Boston cocktail scene was Gertsen's fascination with ice, including the bar's use of 50-pound blocks of crystal-clear ice that are chipped, hewn, and shaved to order. Across the channel is a gem hidden a ways away in South Boston called **Local 149** (149 P Street, South Boston). John Mayer took over the drink program there and brought with him creative sensibilities honed at Craigie on Main. The cocktails there range from inventive to approachable to match the wide assortment of clientele at this neighborhood watering hole. In between the two is the other Franklin, the **Franklin Southie** (152 Dorchester Avenue, Boston). Bar manager Joy Richard, who also manages the Franklin Café and the Citizen Public House, has succeeded in assembling a solid program there as well.

The science lab side of Drink in Fort Point.

Technique

This section is not designed to be a basic primer on drink-making. It is meant to clarify some of the directions in the recipes as well as to impart some of the wisdom I have gained personally by trial and error and by watching the masters at work. For the basics, see my suggestions for books by Robert Hess, Dale DeGroff, and Gary Regan in the introduction.

Measure: I am a big proponent of measuring everything that goes into a drink to get the desired effect of the recipe as written as well as to achieve consistency between drinks. I recommend either a set of jiggers or a graduated mixing cup, such as the ones made by OXO. There are also jiggers made by OXO and Cocktail Kingdom that have handy internal markings to handle smaller volumes. The only other measuring tools needed for these recipes would be a standard barspoon, which is perfect for 1/8 ounce volumes (confirm your tools by filling and pouring into a jigger), and a teaspoon set. The only dry weights in this book are for sugar; luckily, one fluid ounce (2 Tbsp) of sugar weighs pretty much an ounce, so using jiggers for volume will work for weight as well.

Stir: The common rule is that straight spirits drinks (drinks lacking juice, dairy, or eggs) are always stirred, not shaken. The converse is not always true, as there are drinks for which the bartender will stir a recipe containing a tart citrus juice like lemon or lime as a balance for sweetness. When these drinks are stirred, the bartender desires a smoother, silkier texture and not a brighter, livelier tone. To stir a drink, add ice to the ingredients in a mixing glass, then stir with a spoon for 30 to 40 seconds. The minimum amount of ice that will achieve this seems to be three one-inch cubes, if they are cracked into smaller pieces; if not cracked, either more ice or more stirring time will be needed to acquire the proper chilling and dilution. Of course, filling the mixing glass with ice removes these worries. The stirring should be moderate in speed – not fast or violent enough to add air into the drink or splash ice or liquid out of the mixing vessel. The end result will be a drink that is a third larger in volume, such that a three-ounce pre-melt volume becomes around a four-ounce chilled one. Remember, there is no chilling without dilution, since the cooling en-

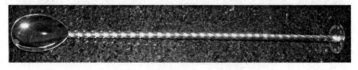

ergy released from ice is the result of it melting from solid to liquid. To pour the chilled drink, a Julep strainer is often used to hold back the ice, but for some mixing vessels, a Hawthorne strainer will work better. A secondary fine-strain step to catch ice shards and other particulates is not as important in a stirred drink as it is in a shaken drink, but some bartenders include it anyways.

Build: Certain drinks are frequently constructed in the serving glass itself. These include some Highballs, Old Fashioneds, and room-temperature cocktails such as Scaffas. Often a quick, gentle stir is necessary for Highballs to disperse the spirits into the mixer. With Old Fashioned-style drinks containing ice, stirring for 15 seconds or so with the ice will get the chill and dilution started. Lastly, room-temperature drinks require only enough stirring to make the mixture homogeneous throughout.

Swizzle: Swizzling is a style of mixing drinks more violent than stirring but more gentle than shaking. It is also often an extension of the built drink mentioned above as the ingredients and crushed ice are added to a tall glass such as a Collins glass or Tiki mug. The traditional mixing implement is a wooden five-pronged swizzle stick called a Bois Lélé that is prepared from a tree found in the Caribbean; these are available through Cocktail Kingdom's online store but are otherwise hard to come by. As a substitute, use a barspoon or a spoon straw; the stereotypical ornamental swizzle sticks will not fit the bill here. In the future, food-safe plastic replicas of the natural ones may become available; Adam Lantheaume of the Boston Shaker is working on a model in conjunction with designer Brian Johnson. To mix the drink, spin the spoon or pronged swizzle stick back and forth between the hands until the drink is chilled; changing the height of the spinning swizzle stick's blades or spoon's bowl will help to quickly chill the drink. With Highball and Collins glasses, the appearance of a frost on the outside of the glass is generally the stopping point.

Shake: Drinks with egg, dairy, muddled fruit, or fruit juices are almost always shaken. Since egg drinks are more complex, there is more about them in the next section. For shaking vessels, the options include the Boston, Parisian, and Cobbler shakers. After adding ice to the ingredients in the shaker of choice, shaking vigorously for 20 seconds or so is sufficient to reach the desired chilling and dilution. Some bartenders choose to do this by feel, stopping when the shaker feels rather cold, but counting seems to be the preferred method. With the Boston or Parisian shaker, the drink is strained out with a Hawthorne strainer; with a Cobbler shaker, the strainer, of course, is built in. Often a secondary straining step is added to catch ice shards, citrus pulp and pips, muddled fruit and herbs, and coarse egg material. For ice shards, a Julep strainer between the shaker and the glass will work in a pinch; however, a mesh strainer is necessary to catch all smaller debris. Finally, in drinks served on the rocks, one approach is to shake and pour unstrained, and the other is to shake and strain into a glass filled with fresh ice; generally the recipes here will specify which the particular bartender opted to do for his or her drink.

Egg Drinks: There are over 60 drinks containing egg white, yolk, or both in this collection. The instructions included with these recipes are written "Shake once without ice and then with ice." For the first or "dry" shake, the rationale is to emulsify the egg proteins into solution. Many bartenders will do this with just the citrus component and add the rest of the ingredients before the second or "wet" shake. The reason is that acids such as citrus juice promote the unfolding of egg proteins, which will cause the egg white portion to foam up when shaken. Sugar will inhibit this initial unfolding and prevent a good foam from forming, but once the foam has formed, sugar will help stabilize it. Many recipes here skip this segregation of ingredients though, and it is not wrong to simplify things

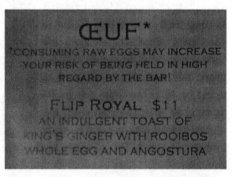

this way; no ill effects will occur if the dry shake is removed either, other than a reduction in the amount of foam and thick mouthfeel. The second shake will contain the rest of the ingredients and ice; this shake is for chilling and dilution purposes similar to the process of making other shaken drinks. The dry shake is often shorter than the wet shake, and 10 seconds or so should be sufficient. I do not recommend dry-shaking egg drinks in

Parisian shakers because they require a vacuum derived from chilled ingredients to seal properly.

Egg Fizz Drinks: One of the bars in town that has Ramos and other Fizzes down to a science is Drink in Fort Point. While the lore of Ramos Gin Fizzes needing to be shaken for many minutes exists, this does not seem to be necessary to get the desired light, fluffy consistency. Drink in its high-volume moments cannot afford that amount of shaking time, so they figured out a solution. Instead of straining the shaken drink into the glass and topping off  with soda water, they add the soda water to the glass and strain into it. This way, the soda water's air bubbles integrate into the drink immediately and less gas is wasted. Next, they add a small amount of extra soda water to the ice inside the strained-out shaker, swirl, and strain or spoon out the light foam on top to add a glorious head to the drink.

Rinse: About two dozen of the recipes in this book include the rinsed glass technique, so I will share my thoughts about it. There are two purposes to rinsing a glass with a spirit. The first is to add a small amount of the ingredient into the flavor profile in a showier way than merely adding it to the mixing glass. The second, more important reason is to coat the exposed sides of a glass with an aromatic ingredient to add to the drink's nose. For rocks glasses and other glasses where the drink does not come up to the top, the technique has the most value. There are two ways of accomplishing a rinse. The most common is to add a small amount, often around a quarter ounce, to the glass; the glass is tilted and slowly rolled, so the insides are completely coated. Often times, the excess is dumped out, but sometimes the bartender chooses to leave the small excess in the glass either to add to the flavor or not be wasteful. The second way is to use a mister and spritz the insides. This technique is certainly faster but it requires a dedicated piece of barware. I could definitely see the home bartender making good use out of an absinthe-filled one, especially if making Sazeracs were a common occurrence. Soon after the rinsing step, the shaken or stirred drink is strained into the glass.

Twist Garnish: A citrus twist garnish is meant to add aromatic oils to the top of the drink, and there are a few variations on this technique. One method is to use a channel knife on the citrus fruit close to the surface of the drink; the mere act of making that ribbon of peel will cast off a lot of oils. The other is to use a vegetable peeler or knife to make a wide twist or a coin, which is squeezed over the drink. From there, the twist can be dropped, floated, or discarded; in the text, the phrase "twist over the top" means that the bartender who made the drink opted to discard the twist, whereas the phrase "garnish with a twist" means that the peel was added to the glass. If the peel is discarded, it is less relevant which twist technique is used. If it is added, the size, shape, and curling will affect the aesthetics of the cocktail. Why add the twist? Two reasons. First, it makes one cocktail appear different from the next, which will break up the monotony especially if you tend toward brown cocktails or other similar looking drinks. Second, it can infuse citrus flavors into the drink over time, such as the lime twist in the Tequila Scaffa. Finally, a handful of recipes in the book call for a flamed twist. By using a lighter or match as a flame source, squeeze the peel through the flame to express the oils on the surface of the drink; some bartenders will often heat the peel before squeezing. While I have heard lore of the oils being caramelized in the flaming process, side-by-side experiments have made me skeptical that there is much difference. One difference is that flaming can add a charred, sulfurous component to the drink if done incorrectly with a match. The match  should be allowed to burn for a bit so that the sulfurous head is burned away. This can be avoided by using the less glamorous cigarette lighter. The heating of the peel can also deposit carbon onto the twist; if it is dropped into the drink, a ring of soot can sometimes be released onto the surface. The only good argument that I have heard for the flamed twist is from Dale DeGroff, who speaks highly about the visual appeal of the burst of fire from igniting the citrus oils; it will make the cocktail the envy of drinkers down the bar by catching their attention. I cannot deny this effect, but otherwise, you have my blessing to ignore the directions to flame a twist and to just use a regular one.

Bitters Garnish: Another popular garnish in the collection is the bitters or liqueur garnish to add both aromatic and visual appeal. The two drinks types that commonly call for it are egg drinks, where the froth will support the bitters, and crushed ice drinks, where the ice will hold the garnish in place. Carefully dribbling out of a dasher bottle, using an eye dropper, or spritzing with a mister are all viable options. One popular technique  with the garnishes for egg or egg white drinks is to carefully deposit the drops on the surface and use a toothpick or thin straw to draw designs through the drops or dashes.

Chilled Glassware: To spare the repetition, I left out the direction to strain into chilled glassware. Clearly, a cold glass will help the drink remain colder for a longer time. The two general methods for chilling glassware are placing the glasses in the freezer and filling the glasses with ice water, with the former being more effective. From experiments that I have done, the difference between using a glass from the freezer and one at room temperature is that the cocktail poured into the freezer-chilled glass will remain colder for five to ten minutes longer than one poured into a room-temperature glass. The downside of the freezer technique is that it requires enough freezer space to include glasses of each type needed. It also requires forethought, because full chilling of the glassware requires about a half hour. An equivalent amount of chilling as the ice water technique can be reached in six to eight minutes in the freezer though. Filling with ice water is more immediate. In about four to five minutes, the glass will come into equilibrium with the ice water; it will not be as effective as freezer-stored glasses, but it is rather a good compromise on time and space constraints. Finally, chilling glassware that will be filled with ice cubes or crushed ice is not all that necessary, although adding soda water to a warm glass will diminish some of its fizz.

The Recipes

❧

505 Drinks from in and around Boston

19th Century Swizzle

Joy Richard was inspired at the Citizen Public House by the return of old-style Jamaican pot-stilled rum.

❖ 1 1/2 oz Smith & Cross Rum
❖ 1/2 oz Green Chartreuse
❖ 1/2 oz Orgeat
❖ 2 oz Pineapple Juice
❖ 1/2 oz Lime Juice

❖ *Build in a Collins glass filled with crushed ice and swizzle to mix and chill. Garnish with 3 dashes of Bittermens Tiki Bitters and 2 cherries, and add a straw.*

◆

#43

Created at Hungry Mother in Cambridge.

❖ 2 oz Old Overholt Rye
❖ 1/2 oz Ferreira Tawny Port
❖ 1/4 oz Maple Syrup
❖ 1 dash Angostura Bitters

❖ *Stir with ice and strain into a rocks glass with a large ice cube. Garnish with an orange twist.*

◆

#47

Created at Hungry Mother in Cambridge.

❖ 1 oz Laird's Applejack
❖ 1 oz Aperol
❖ 1 oz Buffalo Trace Bourbon

❖ *Stir with ice and strain into a rocks glass with a large ice cube.*

◆

#57

Duane Gorey crafted this spiced beer Highball at Hungry Mother in Cambridge.

❖ 3/4 oz Del Maguey Mezcal Vida (or Blanco Tequila)
❖ 3/4 oz Becherovka
❖ 1 oz Lemon Juice
❖ 1/2 oz Simple Syrup

❖ *Shake with ice and strain into a Collins glass filled with ice. Top with 2 oz of Smuttynose Star Island Single (a Belgian-style pale ale) and add a straw.*

# #

#65

A complex Manhattan variation at Hungry Mother in Cambridge.

❖ 2 oz Sazerac 6 Year Rye
❖ 3/4 oz Bonal Gentiane-Quinquina
❖ 1/2 oz Velvet Falernum
❖ 1 dash Fee's Orange Bitters
❖ 1 dash Angostura Bitters

Stir with ice and strain into a rocks glass. Garnish with a cherry.

69 Holland

Hungry Mother in conjunction with Adam Lantheaume made this drink in honor of Adam's cocktail supply store, the Boston Shaker.

❖ 1 oz Plymouth Gin
❖ 1 oz Bols Genever
❖ 3/4 oz Meletti Amaro
❖ 1/2 oz Dry Amontillado Sherry
❖ 2 dash Fee's Peach Bitters

Stir with ice and strain into a cocktail glass. Twist a grapefruit peel over the top.

#72

A Boulevardier riff created at Hungry Mother in Cambridge.

❖ 2 oz Eagle Rare 10 Year Bourbon
❖ 3/4 oz Gran Classico
❖ 1/2 oz Dry Amontillado Sherry

Stir with ice and strain into a glass rinsed with Green Chartreuse. Twist an orange peel over the top.

370 Comm Ave.

Todd Maul's homage to Clio's address in Boston.

❖ 2 oz Beefeater Gin
❖ 1 oz Aperol
❖ 1 oz Lemon Juice
❖ 1/2 oz St. Germain

Shake with ice and strain into a cocktail glass. Optional: garnish with an edible fresh flower petal.

1638

Island Creek Oyster Bar's tribute to the Kopke Winery named after the year the winery was founded.

- ❖ 1 oz Kopke White Port
- ❖ 1 oz Pimm's No. 1
- ❖ 3/4 oz Yellow Chartreuse
- ❖ 2 dash Orange Bitters

❖ *Stir with ice and strain into a coupe*
❖ *glass. Garnish with a lemon twist.*

◆

1795

Craigie on Main's Ted Gallagher developed this variation on Dominic Venegas' 1794.

- ❖ 1 oz Michter's Rye Whiskey
- ❖ 1/2 oz Campari
- ❖ 1/2 oz Aperol
- ❖ 1/2 oz Carpano Sweet Vermouth
- ❖ 1/2 oz Punt e Mes
- ❖ 3 dash Bittermens Mole Bitters

❖ *Stir with ice and strain into a rocks*
❖ *glass filled with fresh ice cubes. Gar-*
❖ *nish with an orange twist and add*
❖ *straws.*

◆

1820

Created by Misty Kalkofen when she was at Drink for the release of Bols Genever.

- ❖ 1 3/4 oz Bols Genever
- ❖ 1/2 oz Lemon Juice
- ❖ 1/2 oz Lavender Syrup
- ❖ 1/4 oz Galliano
- ❖ 1 barspoon Del Maguey Minero Mezcal
- ❖ 1 dash Fee's Whiskey Barrel Bitters

❖ *Shake with ice and strain into a*
❖ *cocktail glass.*

◆

1836

John Mayer named his drink at Craigie on Main in honor of the year Texas declared independence from Mexico.

- ❖ 1 oz Siete Leguas Añejo Tequila
- ❖ 1 oz Campari
- ❖ 1 oz Carpano Sweet Vermouth
- ❖ 2 dash Bittermens Mole Bitters

❖ *Stir with ice and strain into a rocks*
❖ *glass. Add ice cubes and a straw,*
❖ *and garnish with an orange twist.*

# #

1836–1839

Sahil Mehta for Estragon's Spanish Sip event used this war to symbolize the battle between Peru and Chile over who created the Pisco Sour.

❖
❖ 2 oz Macchu Pisco
❖ 1 oz Marie Brizard Apricot Liqueur
❖ 1 oz Lemon Juice
❖ 1 1/2 tsp Marmalade
❖ 1 Egg White
❖
❖ *Shake without ice and then with ice.*
❖ *Strain into a rocks glass and add a*
❖ *straw.*

◆

1910 Cocktail

Drink's Ezra Star riffed on the house classic, the 1919 Cocktail, and made a South of the Border Red Hook-like drink.

❖ 3/4 oz Del Maguey Mezcal Vida
❖ 3/4 oz El Tesoro Reposado Tequila
❖ 1 oz Punt e Mes
❖ 1/2 oz Maraschino Liqueur
❖ 2 dash Peychaud's Bitters
❖
❖ *Stir with ice and strain into a rocks*
❖ *glass. Twist an orange peel over the*
❖ *top.*
❖

3185,
Drink

26

1919 Cocktail

While the Fort Point is the signature cocktail at Drink, Ben Sandrof's 1919 Cocktail took the elements to another level.

❖ 3/4 oz Rittenhouse Rye
❖ 3/4 oz Old Monk Rum
❖ 1 oz Punt e Mes
❖ 1/2 oz Bénédictine
❖ 1 dash Bittermens Mole Bitters

❖ *Stir with ice and strain into a cocktail glass.*

3185

Drink's watermelon-flavored tribute to Beta Cocktail's Gun Shop Fizz named after police codes in New Orleans.

❖ 1 1/2 oz Banks Rum
❖ 1/2 oz Barbancourt Rum
❖ 1/2 oz Aperol
❖ 1/2 oz Honey Syrup
❖ 1/4 oz Gran Classico
❖ 1/4 oz Peychaud's Bitters
❖ 2 inch piece English Cucumber (no peel)

❖ *Cube the cucumber and muddle. Add rest of ingredients and ice, shake, and double strain into a Highball glass containing ice. Top with ~2 oz Reading Lager beer and add a straw.*

Absinthe and Old Lace

Jackson Cannon at Eastern Standard riffed on the classic Grasshopper.

❖ 1 oz Dry Gin
❖ 1/2 oz Absinthe
❖ 1/2 oz Green Crème de Menthe
❖ 1/2 oz Simple Syrup
❖ 1/2 oz Cream
❖ 1 Egg White

❖ *Shake without ice and then with ice. Strain into a cocktail glass, and garnish with either grated dark chocolate or a dash of Bittermens Mole Bitters.*

A Bullet for Fredo

A rather potent but easy to drink tipple crafted by Misty Kalkofen at Brick and Mortar in Cambridge.

- 2 part Nardini Aquavite Bassano Riserva Aged Grappa
- 2 part Perucchi Vermouth Blanc
- 1 part Campari

Compound the mixture for bottling and refrigerate. Serve chilled and undiluted in a small 4-5 oz cocktail glass. Twist a grapefruit peel over the top.

A Few of My Favorite Things

Paul Manzelli conjures up his version of The Sound of Music hit at Bergamot in Somerville.

- 1 1/2 oz Rittenhouse 100 Rye
- 1/2 oz Vergano Americano Chinato
- 1/2 oz Cynar
- 1/2 oz Aperol
- 1 dash Bitter Truth Orange Bitters

Stir with ice and strain into a rocks glass. Garnish with an orange twist.

Agave Maria

A smokey, fruity Lowball with a hint of Fernet's complexity born at the Independent in Somerville.

- 1 1/2 oz Del Maguey Mezcal Vida
- 1 1/2 oz Pineapple Juice
- 3/4 oz Lime Juice
- 1 barspoon Fernet Branca
- 3 dash Peychaud's Bitters
- 1 dash Agave Nectar

Shake with ice and pour unstrained into a rocks glass. Garnish with an orange twist.

Agave Punch

Served at Highland Kitchen in Somerville.

- 2 oz Sauza Tequila
- 1/2 oz Ruby Port
- 1/2 oz Orange Juice
- 1/4 oz Lemon Juice
- 1/4 oz Simple Syrup

Shake with ice and pour into a rocks glass. Garnish with an orange slice.

Agony and Ecstasy

Created by Sam Treadway at Drink such that the imbiber can control the heat of the libation.

❖ 1 oz Del Maguey Mezcal Vida
❖ 1 oz St. Germain
❖ 1 oz Grapefruit Juice

Shake with ice. Add 1 oz ginger beer into the shaker then strain into a rocks glass filled with crushed ice. Garnish with a grapefruit twist decorated with a small line of Chipotle Tabasco Sauce on top, and add straws.

Aku Aku

Carrie Cole's tribute to Easter Island at Craigie on Main in Cambridge.

❖ 1 oz Milagro Blanco Tequila
❖ 1/2 oz Lime Juice
❖ 1/2 oz Pineapple Juice
❖ 1/2 oz Orgeat
❖ 1 barspoon Pastis
❖ 1 small pinch Salt

Shake with ice and strain into a Highball glass containing 1 oz ginger beer and 1 oz soda water. Garnish with a lime wedge and add a straw.

Albert Mathieu

In 2008, there was an Eastern Standard-PDT bartender exchange. While we got PDT's Daniel Eun for a few days, they got Kevin Martin who brought this tribute to the English Channel with him.

❖ 1 1/2 oz Plymouth Gin
❖ 3/4 oz Lillet Blanc
❖ 3/4 oz Green Chartreuse
❖ 1 barspoon St. Germain
❖ 1 dash Regan's Orange Bitters

Stir with ice and strain into a cocktail glass. Garnish with an orange twist.

Alicante

Rendezvous' Scott Holliday was inspired by a Jacques Prévert poem to create this libation for a Grand Marnier event held at Drink in 2009.

- 1 1/2 oz Grand Marnier
- 1 oz Batavia Arrack
- 1 oz Noilly Prat Dry Vermouth
- 2 dash Angostura Orange Bitters
- 2 dash Bittermens Mole Bitters

Build in a rocks glass with a large ice cube. Stir to mix and chill. Add a pinch of salt to the top of the ice cube and flame an orange twist over the top of the drink.

Alfa Sour

A funky Pisco Sour variation from Trina's Starlite Lounge in Somerville.

- 1 1/2 oz Macchu Pisco
- 3/4 oz Grappa
- 3/4 oz Carpano Sweet Vermouth
- 1/2 oz Lemon Juice
- 1 Egg White

Shake without ice and then with ice. Strain into a rocks glass and garnish with 4 drops of Fernet Branca.

Alphonse

Cambridge's Craigie on Main's aperitif tribute to the Art Nouveau painter Alphonse Mucha.

- 1 oz Cocchi Americano
- 3/4 oz Anchor Junipero Gin
- 1/2 oz Carpano Sweet Vermouth
- 1/2 oz Gobelsburger Rosé Wine
- 1/4 oz Cynar
- 1 dash Regan's Orange Bitters

Stir with ice and strain into a cocktail glass.

Alto Cucina

Created by Stephen Shellenberger when he was at Dante in Cambridge.

- 1 oz Scotch
- 1 oz Dry Vermouth
- 1/2 oz St. Germain
- 1/2 oz Cynar

Stir with ice and strain into a cocktail glass. Garnish with an orange twist.

Andorra

Ryan Lotz's tribute at the Hawthorne to independence in the Pyrenees.

- ❖ 1 oz Pierre Ferrand 1840 Cognac
- ❖ 1 oz Lustau Amontillado Sherry
- ❖ 1 oz Nardini Amaro
- ❖ 1 barspoon Rooibos Tea Syrup
- ❖ (or Grenadine)
- ❖ 1 dash Regan's Orange Bitters

❖ *Stir with ice and strain into a coupe*
❖ *glass. Twist a lemon peel over the*
❖ *top.*

Angry Barista

Stoddard's smokey Tiki drink that was perhaps influenced by the Suffering Bar Steward.

◆ 2 oz Dewar's Blended Scotch
❖ 1/2 oz Grapefruit Juice
❖ 1/2 oz Lime Juice
❖ 1/4 oz Cinnamon Syrup
❖ 1/4 oz Fee's Falernum
❖ 1 dash Bittermens Tiki Bitters
❖

❖ *Shake with ice and strain into a*
❖ *rocks glass filled with crushed ice.*
❖ *Garnish with an orange twist and*
❖ *add a straw.*

❖ Alphonse,
❖ Craigie on Main

31

Apotecario

One of Stephen Shellenberger's abstractions of the Negroni that he crafted at Pomodoro in Brookline.

- ❖ 1 oz Cynar
- ❖ 1 oz Martini & Rossi Rosé Vermouth
- ❖ 1 oz Espolón Blanco Tequila
- ❖ 2 dash Peychaud's Bitters

Stir with ice and strain into a cocktail glass.

Applewood

Ryan Lotz's Applejack Old Fashioned variation at Lineage in Brookline; it quickly became his father's favorite cocktail.

- ❖ 2 oz Laird's Applejack
- ❖ 1/2 oz Simple Syrup
- ❖ 1 barspoon St. Elizabeth Allspice Dram
- ❖ 2 dash Angostura Bitters
- ❖ 2 dash Peychaud's Bitters

Stir with ice and strain into a rocks glass rinsed with Laphroaig 10 Year Scotch. Garnish with freshly grated cinnamon.

Aprilia

Kit Paschal's Italian motorcycle tribute at Eastern Standard.

- ❖ 1 oz Beefeater 24 Gin
- ❖ 1 oz Amaro Nonino
- ❖ 1 oz Cocchi Americano
- ❖ 1 dash Bittermens Grapefruit Bitters

Stir with ice and strain into a cocktail glass. Twist a grapefruit peel over the top.

April in Paris

Bergamot's Paul Manzelli crossed the French 75 and the Sidecar and named it after a Count Basie album.

- ❖ 3/4 oz Ansac VS Cognac
- ❖ 3/4 oz Pierre Ferrand Curaçao
- ❖ 3/4 oz Lemon Juice

Shake with ice and strain into a Champagne flute. Top with ~2 oz Louis Bouillot Blanc de Blancs Brut sparkling wine, and twist an orange peel over the top.

Armada

Misty Kalkofen created this tribute to the Anglo-Spanish War at Drink in Boston; the unofficial title was "2 sherry, 2 gin."

- 1 1/2 oz Bols Genever
- 1/2 oz Ransom Old Tom Gin
- 1/2 oz Lustau Dry Oloroso Sherry
- 1/4 oz Lustau Pedro Ximénez Sherry
- 1/4 oz Drambuie

Stir with ice and strain into a cocktail glass. Twist a lemon peel over the top.

Armada

One of the drinks Matt Schrage whipped up for a special restaurant week menu at No. 9 Park in 2009.

- 2 oz Landy VSOP Cognac
- 1 oz Tawny Port
- 1/2 oz Simple Syrup
- 1/4 oz St. Elizabeth Allspice Dram
- 3-4 drop Bittermens Tiki Bitters

Stir with ice and strain into a rocks glass.

Armchair Sailor

Scott Holliday's semi-maritime aperitif at Rendezvous.

- 1 1/2 oz Broadbent Rainwater Madeira
- 3/4 oz Crème Yvette
- 2 dash Scrappy's Celery Bitters

Pour the chilled ingredients (batched and kept in the refrigerator) into a flute glass. Top with ~3 oz of cava.

Assembly Cocktail

Paul Manzelli and Kai Gagnon put together this multi-national drink at Bergamot in Somerville.

- 3/4 oz Pierre Ferrand Cognac
- 3/4 oz Grant "La Garrocha" Amontillado Sherry
- 3/4 oz Drambuie
- 3/4 oz Lemon Juice
- 1/2 barspoon Honey Syrup

Shake with ice and strain into a cocktail glass. Garnish with an orange twist.

❖ Back Word,
❖ Backbar

Autumn Sweater

An Old Fashioned variation created at the Independent in Somerville.

❖ 2 oz Laird's Applejack
❖ 1/4 oz Averna
❖ 1/4 oz Cinzano Sweet Vermouth
❖ 2 dash Bittermens Mole Bitters
❖ 1 Sugar Cube

❖ *Muddle the sugar cube with bitters.*
❖ *Add rest of ingredients and ice, stir,*
❖ *and strain into a rocks glass. Garnish with an orange twist.*

Averna Jimjam

A sweet, herbal, fruity libation by Tom Schlesinger-Guidelli at Eastern Standard.

❖ 1 1/2 oz Averna
❖ 3/4 oz Lemon Juice
❖ 3/4 oz Marie Brizard Apry

❖ *Shake with ice and strain into a*
❖ *cocktail glass.*

Avery's Arrack-ari

The Bittermens' Avery Glasser had a hand in this Green Street recipe.

- ❖ 1 1/2 oz Batavia Arrack
- ❖ 1/2 oz Lime Juice
- ❖ 1/2 oz Simple Syrup

❖ *Shake with ice and strain into a cocktail coupe rinsed with Talisker 10 Year Scotch. Garnish with a lime wedge.*

Aztec Conquest

Originally created with Bittermens Taza Chocolate Extract for the label recipe contest, Ryan Lotz later switched to their mole bitters for Lineage's menu.

- ❖ 1 1/2 oz Berkshire Mountain Bourbon
- ❖ 3/4 oz Lustau East India Solera Sherry
- ❖ 1/2 oz Combier Orange Liqueur
- ❖ 1 dash Bittermens Mole Bitters

❖ *Stir with ice and strain into a rocks glass. Twist an orange peel over the top.*

Back Word

A Last Word variation by Joe Cammarata and Sam Treadway at Backbar that makes good use of the syrup in cherry jars.

- ❖ 1 1/2 oz Oxley Gin
- ❖ 3/4 oz Yellow Chartreuse
- ❖ 1/2 oz Lillet Blanc
- ❖ 1/4 oz Luxardo Cherry Jar Syrup
- ❖ 1 dash Bitter Truth Lemon Bitters

❖ *Stir with ice and strain into a coupe glass. Garnish with a lemon peel boat impaled by a short sprig of rosemary.*

Balao Swizzle

Crafted by Corey Bunnewith at Coppa for the Vinos de Jerez Cocktail Competition in 2009.

- ❖ 3 oz Dry Oloroso Sherry
- ❖ 1/2 oz Velvet Falernum
- ❖ 1/2 oz Averna (or similar amaro)
- ❖ 3/4 oz Lime Juice
- ❖ 1/2 tsp Toasted Caraway Seeds

❖ *Muddle toasted caraway seeds in a Collins glass to extract oils; discard the seeds. Add all liquid ingredients, fill with crushed ice, and swizzle. Garnish with a barspoon of Angostura Bitters and add a straw.*

Bamboo Crusta

Fred Yarm's variation of the classic Bamboo Cocktail that was inspired by Scott Holliday's love of the Crusta.

- ❖ 1 oz Dry Sherry
- ❖ 1 oz Dry Vermouth
- ❖ 1/4 oz Triple Sec
- ❖ 1/4 oz Maraschino Liqueur
- ❖ 1/4 oz Lemon Juice
- ❖ 1 dash Orange Bitters
- ❖ 1 dash Angostura Bitters

❖ *Shake with ice and strain into a small wineglass with a sugar-coated rim. Garnish with a wide lemon peel looped around the inside of the glass' opening.*

◆

Barbados Fix

An old school drink style brought back by Fred Yarm during National Rum Week, 2011.

- ❖ 1 1/2 Barbados Rum
- ❖ 1 oz Lime Juice
- ❖ 1/2 oz Passion Fruit Syrup
- ❖ 1/2 oz Earl Grey Tea Syrup

❖ *Shake with ice and strain into a rocks glass filled with crushed ice. Garnish with lime slices and/or berries in season. Add a straw.*

◆

Bartender on Acid

After hearing a customer's unfulfilled request at Drink for a Surfer on Acid, Fred Yarm later suggested the Drink version, and it turned out to sell well there.

- ❖ 1 oz Fernet Branca
- ❖ 1 oz Smith & Cross Rum
- ❖ 1 oz Pineapple Juice

❖ *Shake with ice and strain into rocks glass.*

◆

Battle of Trafalgar

Aaron Butler's English history degree shines through in his Russell House Tavern drink.

- ❖ 1 oz Pimm's No. 1
- ❖ 3/4 oz St. Germain
- ❖ 3/4 oz Batavia Arrack
- ❖ 1/2 oz Lime Juice
- ❖ 1/2 oz Honey Syrup

❖ *Shake with ice and strain into a rocks glass. Twist an orange peel over the drink.*

Battle Royal Fizz

A challenging egg drink from Ben Sandrof's Sunday Salon speakeasy series.

❖ 1 1/4 oz Cynar
❖ 1 1/4 oz Fernet Branca
❖ 1/2 oz Brown Sugar Syrup
❖ 1 dash Angostura Bitters
❖ 1 Whole Egg

Shake without ice and then with ice. Strain into a rocks glass filled with 1 oz Gritty's Blackfly Stout.

◆

Beach Cruiser

Citizen's Chad Arnholt made this Painkiller-like drink in tribute to the Fernet Branca bicycles that many bartenders in town were gifted.

❖ 1 oz Zaya Gran Reserva Rum
❖ 3/4 oz Fernet Branca
❖ 1/2 oz Falernum
❖ 1 oz Coco Lopez Cream of Coconut
❖ 1 oz Orange Juice
❖ 1/2 oz Lime Juice

Shake with ice and strain into a rocks glass filled with crushed ice. Garnish with a few dashes of Tiki Bitters and add straws.

◆

Beergria

This amazing beer Sangria was created at Trina's Starlite Lounge in Somerville.

❖ 3/4 oz Laird's 7 1/2 Year Apple Brandy
❖ 3/4 oz Carpano Sweet Vermouth
❖ 1/2 oz Apricot Liqueur
❖ 1 oz Orange Juice
❖ 1/2 oz Lemon Juice
❖ 1/2 oz Simple Syrup

Shake with ice and strain into a pint glass. Top with around 10 oz Clown Shoes Clementine Witbier and stir gently to mix. Garnish with an orange wedge.

Bee Sting

Misty Kalkofen's variation of a Bee's Knees made for the Beefeater 24 release party at Drink in 2009.

❖ 2 oz Beefeater 24 Gin
❖ 1/2 oz Lemon Juice
❖ 1/2 oz Honey Syrup
❖ 12 Peppercorns
❖

❖ *Muddle peppercorns in shaker. Add*
❖ *rest of ingredients and ice, shake,*
❖ *and double strain into a cocktail*
❖ *glass.*

Belle de Jour

One of the early sparklers at Eastern Standard in Boston.

◆ 1/2 oz Cognac
❖ 1/2 oz Bénédictine
❖ 1/2 oz Grenadine
❖ 1/2 oz Lemon Juice

❖ *Shake with ice and strain into a*
❖ *Champagne flute. Top with 2-3 oz*
❖ *dry sparkling wine and garnish*
◆ *with a lemon twist.*

Beneficio de Café

Misty Kalkofen designed this cocktail at Drink for her mezcal talk at Portland's Cocktail Week in 2011.

❖ 1 1/2 oz Del Maguey Mezcal Vida
❖ 1 oz Averna
❖ 1/4 oz Dark Muscovado Syrup
❖ 1/4 oz Bénédictine
❖ 2 dash Angostura Bitters
❖

❖ *Stir with ice and strain into a cock-*
❖ *tail coupe. Garnish with freshly*
❖ *grated dark roast coffee beans. In a*
❖ *pinch, maple syrup has been used in*
◆ *place of the muscovado syrup.*

Bentiki Fizz

A tropical improvisation by Ben Sandrof at his Sunday Salon speakeasy series.

❖ 1 oz Ron Matusalem Classico Rum
❖ 1 oz Pierre Ferrand Ambre Cognac
❖ 1/2 oz Lemon Juice
❖ 1/2 oz Grapefruit Juice
❖ 1/2 oz Orgeat
❖ 1/2 oz Cinnamon Syrup
❖ 1 Egg White

❖ *Shake with ice and strain into a*
❖ *Highball glass. Top with ~2 oz soda*
❖ *water and twist a grapefruit peel*
❖ *over the top. Garnish with 3 drops of*
❖ *Tiki Bitters and add a straw.*

Bikini Atoll

Bikini Atoll

Fred Yarm's cross of a Nuclear Daiquiri and a Mai Tai.

1 oz Wray & Nephew Overproof White Rum
1/2 oz Green Chartreuse
1/2 oz Velvet Falernum
1/2 oz Triple Sec
1/2 oz Orgeat
1 oz Lime Juice

Shake with ice and strain into a rocks glass filled with crushed ice and a spent half lime shell. Add a straw and garnish with mint sprigs.

Bird Bath

A collaborative effort of Carrie Cole and the Bittermens' Avery and Janet Glasser at Craigie on Main using three bird-themed ingredients.

2 oz Cocchi Americano
1 oz Scarlet Ibis Rum
1/2 oz Fighting Cock Bourbon

Stir with ice and strain into a coupe glass.

39

Bishop Allen

A cocktail created by Fred Yarm for Green Street's Stout Sunday menu.

1 1/2 oz Appleton Reserve Rum
1/2 oz Falernum
1/2 oz Pineapple Juice
1/4 oz Lime Juice

Shake with ice and strain into a wine or rocks glass containing 1 1/2 oz of stout beer.

Bittah Walshie

Ryan McGrale made a tribute to Stoddard's Jamie Walsh and it later appeared on Stoddard's menu.

2 oz Plymouth Gin
3/4 oz Angostura Bitters
1/2 oz Lime Juice
1/2 oz Orgeat
1/4 oz Curaçao

Shake with ice and strain into a coupe glass.

Bitter End

Created at Highland Kitchen in Somerville.

1 1/2 oz Gordon's Dry Gin
1/2 oz Cointreau
1/2 oz Cynar
3/4 oz Grapefruit Juice
2 dash Fee's Grapefruit Bitters

Shake with ice and pour unstrained into a rocks glass.

Bitter Fling

Ben Sandrof served this drink at his Sunday Salon speakeasy series.

1 1/2 oz Berkshire Mountain Greylock Gin
1/2 oz Aperol
1/2 oz Yellow Chartreuse
1/2 oz Lemon Juice
1 dash Aromatic or Floral Bitters

Shake with ice and strain into a cocktail glass. Garnish with a grapefruit twist.

Bitter in Brazil

Created at Worcester's Citizen Restaurant.

❖ 1 1/2 oz Cabana Cachaça
❖ 3/4 oz Grand Marnier
❖ 1/2 oz Punt e Mes
❖ 1/4 oz Simple Syrup
❖
❖ *Stir with ice and strain into a rocks glass rinsed with Fernet Branca. Garnish with a lemon twist.*

◆

Bittersweet Serenade

A nutty interplay of sherry and walnut liqueur by Sahil Mehta at Estragon in Boston.

❖ 1 oz Lustau Los Arcos Dry Amontillado Sherry
❖ 1 oz Philippe Latourelle Calvados
❖ 1 oz Nux Alpina Walnut Liqueur
❖ 1 dash Angostura Bitters
❖
❖ *Stir with ice and strain into a cocktail glass. Garnish with an orange twist.*

◆

Black Cadillac

A Flip created by Ryan Lotz at Lineage in Brookline.

❖ 3 oz Bar Harbor's Cadillac Mountain Stout
❖ 1/2 oz Laphroaig 10 Year Scotch
❖ 1/2 oz Smith & Cross Rum
❖ 1/2 oz Simple Syrup
❖ 1 Whole Egg

❖ *Shake without ice and then with ice. Garnish with 9 drops of Fee's Whiskey Barrel Bitters.*

◆

Black Friar

For a Plymouth Gin cocktail contest, Fred Yarm crafted this Frisco-like recipe.

❖ 1 1/2 oz Plymouth Gyn
❖ 1/2 oz Bénédictine
❖ 1/2 oz Cocchi Americano
❖ 1/2 oz Lemon Juice
❖ 1 dash Angostura Bitters
❖
❖ *Shake with ice and strain into a cocktail glass. Garnish with a lemon twist.*
❖

Blonde on Blonde

Rendezvous' Scott Holiday named his lightly colored cocktail after a Bob Dylan song.

- 3/4 oz Yellow Chartreuse
- 3/4 oz Pisco
- 3/4 oz Lemon Juice
- 3/4 oz White Port

Shake with ice and strain into a cocktail glass.

Blue Parrot

One of Eastern Standard's Tikisms concocted to use up a case of blue liqueur bought for a 4th of July red, white, and blue-themed post-Valentine's Day industry event.

- 1 oz Batavia Arrack
- 1 oz El Dorado White Rum
- 1/2 oz Grand Marnier
- 1/2 oz Bols Blue Curaçao
- 1/2 oz Lemon Juice

Shake with ice and strain into a highball glass filled with crushed ice. Float 1/2 oz Henri Bardouin Pastis, add a straw, and garnish with a wide lemon twist. Sub regular Curaçao and a drop of blue food coloring for the Blue Curaçao.

Bohemian, Green Street

Bohannon

Created by Casey Keenan at Deep Ellum in Allston.

- 2 oz Plymouth Gin
- 1/2 oz Green Chartreuse
- 1/2 oz Swedish Punsch

Stir with ice and strain into a cocktail glass. Garnish with a pinch of freshly ground black pepper.

Bohemian

Misty Kalkofen came up with the Bohemian in 2008 and it quickly became the most popular St. Germain drink at Green Street.

- 1 oz Beefeater Gin
- 1 oz St. Germain
- 1 oz Pink Grapefruit Juice
- 1 dash Peychaud's Bitters

Shake with ice and strain into a cocktail glass.

Bold Proposition

A Matt Schrage creation at No. 9 Park in Boston.

- 1 1/2 oz Hayman's Old Tom Gin
- 3/4 oz Zirbenz Stone Pine Liqueur
- 3/4 oz Punt e Mes

Stir with ice and strain into a rocks glass rinsed with Laphroaig 10 Year Scotch.

Bonita Applebum

Emma Hollander of Trina's Starlite Lounge offered her A Tribe Called Quest tribute for a Fernet Branca industry night at the Franklin Southie.

- 1 oz Laird's Applejack
- 3/4 oz Fernet Branca
- 3/4 oz Drambuie

Stir with ice and strain into a rocks glass. Garnish with an orange twist.

Bosc Word

Scott Holliday mixed this pear-flavored Last Word riff at Rendezvous in Cambridge.

- 3/4 oz Beefeater Gin
- 3/4 oz Lime Juice
- 3/4 oz Mathilde Pear Liqueur
- 3/4 oz Aperol

Shake with ice and strain into a cocktail glass.

BO

Boston Bog

A vodka drink at Stoddard's that works so much better with gin.

❖ 1 1/2 oz Beefeater Gin
❖ 1/2 oz Plymouth Sloe Gin
❖ 1 1/2 oz Cranberry Juice
❖ 1/4 oz Ginger Syrup

Shake with ice and strain into a rocks glass filled with crushed ice. Garnish with 4 fresh cranberries and add straws.

◆

Boston Molassacre

A Flip designed by Eastern Standard's Kit Paschal and dubbed after the 1919 disaster.

❖ 1 oz Smith & Cross Rum
❖ 1/2 oz Zacapa 23 Year Rum
❖ 1/2 oz Cruzan Black Strap Rum
❖ 1/2 oz Orgeat
❖ 1 barspoon St. Elizabeth Allspice Dram
❖ 1 Whole Egg

Shake without ice and then with ice. Strain into a coupe glass.

◆

Bourbon & Birch

An herbal nightcap from Bergamot in Somerville.

❖ 1 1/2 oz Old Weller Antique Bourbon
❖ 1 oz Amaro Nonino
❖ 1/2 oz Root Liqueur

Stir with ice and strain into a rocks glass. Garnish with a grapefruit twist.

◆

Bourbon Belle

At Tremont 647, Joy Richard created what later became her LUPEC Boston moniker.

❖ 2 oz Buffalo Trace Bourbon
❖ 1/2 oz Mathilde Peach Liqueur
❖ 1/2 oz Carpano Sweet Vermouth
❖ 2 dash Angostura Bitters

Stir with ice and strain into a cocktail glass garnished with a brandied cherry.

Bourbon Derby Flip

Eastern Standard's egg-laden tribute to the ponies.

- ❖ 3/4 oz Four Roses Bourbon
- ❖ 3/4 oz Lustau East India Solera Sherry
- ❖ 3/4 oz Aged Rum
- ❖ 1/2 oz Cinnamon Syrup
- ❖ 1/2 oz Cream
- ❖ 1 Whole Egg

- ❖ *Shake without ice and then with ice.*
- ❖ *Strain into a coupe glass.*

Bourbon Rumba

Deep Ellum's riff on the Brown Rumba from the 1937 Café Royal Cocktail Book.

- ◆ 1 3/4 oz Old Fitzgerald Bourbon
- ❖ 3/4 oz Pineapple Syrup
- ❖ 3/4 oz Lemon Juice
- ❖ 1 Egg White
- ❖ 1 dash Aromatic Bitters

- ❖ *Shake without ice and then with ice.*
- ❖ *Strain into a rocks glass, and twist a*
- ❖ *lemon peel over the top.*

Boutonnière

A floral take on the Marconi Wireless by Scott Holliday at Rendezvous in Cambridge.

- ◆ 2 oz Laird's Applejack
- ❖ 1 oz Dry Vermouth
- ❖ 1/2 oz St. Germain
- ❖ 1 dash Peychaud's Bitters
- ❖ 1 dash Orange Bitters

- ❖ *Stir with ice and strain into a cock-*
- ❖ *tail glass. Garnish with an orange*
- ◆ *twist.*

Bramble and Arabica

A gorgeous coffee and berry Flip created at Craigie on Main in Cambridge.

- ❖ 1 oz Privateer Amber Rum
- ❖ 1 oz Punt e Mes
- ❖ 1/4 oz Coffee Liqueur
- ❖ 1/4 oz Simple Syrup
- ❖ 1 barspoon Crème de Mûre
- ❖ 1 pinch Salt
- ❖ 2 dash Angostura Bitters
- ❖ 1 Whole Egg

- ❖ *Shake without ice and then with ice.*
- ❖ *Strain into a coupe glass and gar-*
- ❖ *nish with a dusting of fine espresso coffee grounds.*

Bristol

Will Quackenbush's spicy riff on the Alaska at Highland Kitchen in Somerville.

2 oz Old Overholt Rye
3/4 oz Yellow Chartreuse
1/4 oz St. Elizabeth Allspice Dram
1 dash Fee's Chocolate Bitters

Stir with ice and strain into a cocktail glass. Garnish with an orange twist.

Brooklyn Brawler

A more aggressive variation of the Brooklyn created by Misty Kalkofen at Drink.

1 1/2 oz Old Overholt Rye
1/2 oz Punt e Mes
1/2 oz Averna
1 barspoon Luxardo Maraschino Liqueur

Stir with ice and strain into a cocktail glass. Twist an orange peel over the drink.

Buckminster

Created at Highland Kitchen in Somerville.

1 1/2 oz Gordon's Gin
3/4 oz Maurin Quina
3/4 oz Lillet Blanc
2 dash Fee's Orange Bitters

Stir with ice and strain into a cocktail glass. Garnish with an orange twist.

Bull Rider

Jason at Rendezvous took the classic Brave Bull to another level.

1 1/2 oz Luna Azul Reposado Tequila
3/4 oz Kahlua Coffee Liqueur
1/2 oz S. Maria al Monte Amaro

Stir with ice and pour unstrained into a rocks glass. Garnish with a wide lemon twist and add straws.

Burlington

Created by Chad Arnholt of the Citizen Public House in Boston.

- 2 1/2 oz Old Overholt Rye Whiskey
- 3/4 oz Punt e Mes
- 2 tsp Simple Syrup
- 1 tsp Maple Syrup
- 1 pinch Smoked Salt (1/20 tsp)

Stir with ice and strain into a rocks glass.

Bustamante

Craigie on Main's John Mayer won the Appleton mixology contest in 2010 with this tribute to Jamaica's first prime minister.

- 1 1/2 oz Appleton Reserve Rum
- 3/4 oz Campari
- 1/2 oz Sherry
- 3/8 oz Bénédictine
- 2 dash Regan's Orange Bitters

Stir with ice and strain into a cocktail glass. Garnish with an orange twist.

Bristol,
Highland Kitchen

CA

Calabura Flip

A Flip by Ryan Lotz at Lineage named after the Jamaican Cherry Tree.

2 oz Smith & Cross Rum
1/2 oz Cherry Heering
1/2 oz Angostura Bitters
1 oz Simple Syrup
1 Whole Egg

Shake without ice and then with ice. Strain into a rocks glass and garnish with a few drops of Fee's Whiskey Barrel Bitters.

Caledonian

An elegant smokey Highball by Naomi Levy at Eastern Standard.

2 oz Dewar's Blended Scotch
1 oz Rooibos Tea Syrup
1/2 oz Lemon Juice
1/4 oz Orange Juice
6 drop St. Elizabeth Allspice Dram

Shake with ice and strain into a Highball glass filled with fresh ice. Top with 1 oz sparkling wine and add a straw.

Calla Lily

Paul Manzelli's Chrysanthemum-like ode to Spring at Bergamot in Somerville.

1 1/2 oz Perucchi Dry Vermouth
1/2 oz Lillet Blanc
1/2 oz Bénédictine
1/2 oz Lemon Juice
2 dash Herbsaint

Shake with ice and strain into a wine glass.

Cambridge-port

Derric Crothers' Manhattan variation tribute to Green Street's neighborhood.

2 oz Rittenhouse 100 Rye
1/2 oz Taylor Fladgate Ruby Port
1/2 oz Yellow Chartreuse

Stir with ice and strain into a cocktail coupe. Garnish with a grapefruit twist.

Camino Cocktail

Crafted by Tom Schlesinger-Guidelli for the inaugural Craigie on Main cocktail menu.

❖ 1 1/2 oz Rittenhouse 100 Rye
❖ 1 oz Amber Vermouth (sub Sweet Vermouth)
❖ 1/2 oz Mirto
❖ 1 dash Regan's Orange Bitters
❖ 1 dash Angostura Bitters

Stir with ice and strain into a rocks glass. Garnish with a flamed orange twist.

Canboulay

A smokey straight spirits drink named after the burning of the sugar cane fields before harvest and created by Jared Sadoian at Craigie on Main.

◆ 3/4 oz Scarlet Ibis Rum
❖ 3/4 oz Bowmore Islay Scotch
❖ 3/4 oz Averna
❖ 1/2 oz Barolo Chinato
❖ 1/4 oz Simple Syrup
❖ 2 dash Bittermens Mole Bitters

Stir with ice and strain into a rocks glass rinsed with Del Maguey Chichicapa Mezcal. Twist an orange peel over the top.

Can Can

A LUPEC Boston original served at a Chartreuse event at Green Street in 2007.

◆ 5 Sour Cherries
❖ 1 oz Yellow Chartreuse
❖ 1/4 oz Grapefruit Juice
❖ 1 dash Angostura Bitters

Muddle the cherries in the bottom of a mixing glass. Add rest of ingredients, shake with ice, and double strain into a Champagne flute. Top with Nino Franco Prosecco.

Cantante Para Mi Vida

Drink bartender California Gold served her take on Tequila Por Mi Amante at a Pernod Absinthe Bar Crawl in 2010.

◆ 3/4 oz Pernod Absinthe
❖ 3/4 oz Strawberry Syrup
❖ 1/2 oz Lemon Juice
❖ 1/2 oz Del Maguey Mezcal Vida
❖ 1 barspoon Orgeat
❖ 1/2 oz Egg White

Shake without ice and then with ice. Strain into a glass, top with ~1 oz soda water, and add a straw.

❖ Carlota's Tears,
❖ Russell House
❖ Tavern

Carletti

Eastern Standard's Hugh Fiore demonstrated how well Campari and chocolate pair together.

❖ 1 1/2 oz Death's Door Gin
❖ 3/4 oz Campari
❖ 3/4 oz Crème de Cacao
❖ 1 dash Bittermens Boston Bittahs
❖
❖ *Stir with ice and strain into a rocks*
❖ *glass rinsed with Rothman & Winter*
❖ *Apricot Liqueur. Garnish with a*
❖ *lemon twist.*

Carlota's Tears

Influenced by Misty Kalkofen's Maximilian Affair, Russell House Tavern's Aaron Butler named this after Maximilian's wife.

❖ 2 oz Milagro Silver Tequila
❖ 3/4 oz Lime Juice
❖ 3/4 oz Velvet Falernum
❖ 1/2 oz Pernod Absinthe
❖ 1 dash Angostura Orange Bitters
❖
❖ *Shake with ice and strain into a*
❖ *coupe glass.*

Carnivale

Eastern Standard's Kevin Martin won a pisco competition with this recipe.

❖ 1 1/2 oz Pisco
❖ 3/4 oz Campari
❖ 3/4 oz Maraschino Liqueur
❖ 1 dash Bittermens Mole Bitters

Stir with ice and strain into a cocktail glass. Garnish with an orange twist.

◆

Carthusian Sour

A Chartreuse egg white Sour created at Deep Ellum in Allston.

❖ 1 1/2 oz Old Overholt Rye
❖ 3/4 oz Green Chartreuse
❖ 1/2 oz Lemon Juice
❖ 1/2 oz Simple Syrup
❖ 1 dash Angostura Bitters
❖ 1 Egg White

Shake without ice and then with ice. Strain into a rocks glass, and twist a lemon peel over the top.

◆

Casino Imperial

A great multi-tiered sparkler from Tom Schlesinger-Guidelli at Craigie on Main in Cambridge.

❖ 4 oz Sparkling Wine
❖ 1 oz Calvados
❖ 1 Sugar Cube
❖ A few dashes Herbsaint
❖ Large Lemon Peel

In a mixing glass, soak the sugar cube in Herbsaint. Partially fill a Champagne flute with sparkling wine and drop the Herbsaint-soaked sugar cube and the large lemon twist into the flute. Float the ounce of Calvados.

◆

Cedric's Chartreuse Smash

At Silvertone, if Cedric Adam's name is associated with a drink, there is a good chance it contains Green Chartreuse.

❖ 2 oz Green Chartreuse
❖ 3/4 oz Lime Juice
❖ 1/2 oz Simple Syrup
❖ 6 leaf Mint

Muddle mint leaves with simple syrup. Add rest of the ingredients and shake with ice. Double strain into a rocks glass filled with crushed ice and garnish with a mint sprig.

CE

Cell #34

Served by Ben Sandrof at his Sunday Salon speakeasy series.

❖ 1 oz Beefeater Gin
❖ 1 oz Campari
❖ 1 oz St. Germain
❖ 2 dash Peychaud's Bitters

Stir with ice and strain into a rocks glass. Garnish with a lemon twist.

◆

Central Carré

Scott Holliday's tribute to Rendezvous Central Square location was based off of the classic Vieux Carré.

❖ 1 oz Bols Genever
❖ 1 oz Cognac
❖ 1 oz Punt e Mes
❖ 1 barspoon Fernet Branca

Stir with ice and strain into a cocktail glass.

◆

César Moro

Fred Yarm's submission to the Saveur Cointreau contest in honor of a Peruvian surrealist.

❖ 1 1/2 oz Pisco
❖ 1/2 oz Cointreau
❖ 1/2 oz Pineapple Juice
❖ 1/2 oz Dry Vermouth
❖ 1 dash Fee's Whiskey Barrel Bitters

Shake with ice and strain into a cocktail glass. Garnish with an orange twist.

◆

Ce Soir

Created by Nicole Lebedevitch at the Hawthorne in Boston.

❖ 1 1/2 oz Pierre Ferrand 1840 Cognac
❖ 3/4 oz Cynar
❖ 1/2 oz Yellow Chartreuse
❖ 2 dash Regan's Orange Bitters

Stir with ice and strain into a rocks glass. Twist a lemon peel over the top.

Chappaquid-dick

Eastern Standard's Kevin Martin named his Tikism after one of the tranquil island paradises in Massachusetts. Perfect for a Daiquiri time out!

- ❖ 1 oz Berkshire Mountain Rum
- ❖ 1 oz Ron Bermudez Rum
- ❖ 1 oz Lime Juice
- ❖ 1/2 oz Honey Syrup
- ❖ 1/2 oz Falernum
- ❖ 1 dash Bittermens Tiki Bitters

❖ *Shake with ice and strain into a cocktail coupe glass. Garnish with freshly grated nutmeg.*

Chee Hoo Fizz

Tiki fanatic Randy Wong's Fizz that got served quite often at Tiki Sundays at Drink.

- ❖ 1 1/2 oz Pierre Ferrand Cognac
- ❖ 1/2 oz Lime Juice
- ❖ 1/2 oz Orgeat
- ❖ 1/2 oz Velvet Falernum
- ❖ 4 dash Peychaud's Bitters
- ❖ 1 Egg White

❖ *Shake without ice and then with ice. Strain into a Highball glass and top with ~2 oz soda water. Garnish with a wide lime twist and add a straw.*

Chica Facil

An easy drinking Margarita variation from the Lone Star Taco Bar in Allston.

- ❖ 2 oz Blanco Tequila
- ❖ 3/4 oz Aperol
- ❖ 3/4 oz Lime Juice
- ❖ 1/4 oz Agave Nectar
- ❖ 1 dash Orange Bitters

❖ *Shake with ice and strain into a rocks glass. Squeeze a lime wedge over the top and drop in.*

Chocolate Flip

It is the milk stout that makes Kevin Martin's Flip at Eastern Standard shine.

- ❖ 1 1/2 oz Cruzan Blackstrap Rum
- ❖ 1/2 oz Crème de Cacao
- ❖ 1/2 oz Simple Syrup
- ❖ 1 Whole Egg

❖ *Shake without ice and then with ice. Strain into a coupe glass and top with 1 1/2 oz Left Hand Milk Stout. Garnish with grated chocolate.*

CH

Christmas Goose

Peter Cipriani's drink offering at a Bols Genever industry event at the Franklin.

2 oz Bols Genever
1/2 oz Plymouth Sloe Gin
1/2 oz Bénédictine
3 dash Jerry Thomas Decanter Bitters

Stir with ice and strain into a cocktail glass.

Christmas Grouse

Green Street's Derric Crothers created this cocktail for the holidays.

2 oz Famous Grouse Scotch
1/2 oz Zirbenz Stone Pine Liqueur
1/2 oz Bärenjäger Honey Liqueur

Stir with ice and strain into a cocktail coupe. Garnish with a lemon twist.

Chronic Iced Tea

A favorite from the defunct B Side Lounge in Cambridge that found its way on to the Green Street menu.

1 oz Pierre Ferrand Ambre Cognac
1 oz Bärenjäger Honey Liqueur
1/2 oz Lemon Juice

Shake with ice and pour unstrained into a pint glass. Top with 3-4 oz Earl Grey iced tea, garnish with a lemon wheel, and add a straw.

Chupacabra

A cryptozoological wonder from The Gallows in Boston.

1 oz Lunazul Reposado Tequila
1 oz St. Germain
1/2 oz Punt e Mes
1/2 oz Lime Juice
1 barspoon Mezcal

Shake with ice and strain into a cocktail glass. Garnish with a lime wheel.

Chupacabra,
The Gallows

Cinnamon Collins

Created by Ben Sandrof and served at his Sunday Salon speakeasy series.

❖ 1 1/2 oz Cognac
❖ 1/2 oz Hartley & Gibson Amontillado Sherry
❖ 1/2 oz Lemon Juice
❖ 1/2 oz Cinnamon Syrup

❖ *Shake with ice and strain into a Collins glass filled with ice. Top with ~2 oz ginger beer, and add a straw. Garnish with a few dashes of Angostura Bitters and an orange twist.*

City of Eternal Spring

Aaron Butler crafted this hibiscus-infused tequila drink at Russell House Tavern and named it after a popular vacation spot in Mexico.

❖ 1 oz Gran Centenario Rosangel Tequila
❖ 3/4 oz St. Germain
❖ 3/4 oz Meletti Amaro
❖ 1/2 oz Lemon Juice
❖ 2 dash Bittermens Grapefruit Bitters

❖ *Shake with ice and strain into a coupe glass. Optional: garnish with a hibiscus petal.*

55

CO

Cocktail Miranda

Created by Misty Kalkofen at Green Street.

❖ 2 oz Old Overholt Rye Whiskey
❖ 1/2 oz Apricot Liqueur
❖ 1/2 oz Averna

❖ Stir with ice and strain into a cocktail glass.

Cold Blooded Fashion

One of Misty Kalkofen's beer cocktail for a Spin the Bottle event at Brick and Mortar featuring Chris Lohring of Notch Brewing.

❖ 1 1/2 oz Bols Genever
❖ 3/4 oz Orange Juice
❖ 1/4 oz Simple Syrup
❖ 1 dash Fee's Whiskey Barrel Bitters

❖ Shake with ice and strain into a rocks glass containing ice cubes. Top with ~2 oz Notch Saison beer and give a quick stir.

Cold Emerald Punch

A refreshing take on Jerry Thomas' Cold Ruby Punch by Fred Yarm.

❖ 1 oz Cachaça
❖ 1 oz Lillet Blanc
❖ 1 1/2 oz Green Tea (cooled)
❖ 1/2 oz (1 Tbsp) Sugar
❖ 3/8 oz Lemon Juice
❖ 1/8 oz Pineapple Juice

❖ Stir sugar with tea and juices until dissolved. Add rest of ingredients and ice, shake, and strain into a rocks glass.

Comanche Club

No. 9 Park's Ted Kilpatrick concocted this "4 parts Negroni, 3 parts Last Word" for a J.D. Salinger-themed charity event at the Hawthorne in 2012.

❖ 1 1/24 oz Gin
❖ 2/3 oz Sweet Vermouth
❖ 2/3 oz Campari
❖ 3/8 oz Green Chartreuse
❖ 3/8 oz Maraschino Liqueur
❖ 3/8 oz Lime Juice

❖ Shake with ice and strain into a cocktail glass.

Coney Island

A chocolatey take on a Manhattan by Fred Yarm.

- ❖ 2 oz Rye Whiskey
- ❖ 1/2 oz Punt e Mes
- ❖ 1/2 oz Crème de Cacao
- ❖ 1 dash Angostura Bitters
- ❖
- ❖ *Stir with ice and strain into a cocktail glass. Garnish with a cherry.*

Coney Island Strong Man

A stunning beer cocktail by Courtney Bissonnette at Coppa in Boston.

- ❖ 1 oz Green Chartreuse
- ❖ 1 oz Yellow Chartreuse
- ❖ 3/4 oz Lemon Juice
- ❖
- ❖ *Shake with ice and strain into a pint glass. Add 7 oz of Miller High Life beer, and top with ice cubes. Garnish with a lemon wheel.*

Contessa

Part of the Flight of Heraldry along with the Negroni and Patrician created by Ben Gertsen, Ryan McGrale, and Courtney Bissonnette at No. 9 Park.

- ❖ 1 oz Beefeater Gin
- ❖ 1 oz Aperol
- ❖ 1 oz Noilly Prat Dry Vermouth
- ❖
- ❖ *Stir with ice and strain into a cocktail glass. Garnish with an orange or lemon twist.*
- ❖

Coolidge

Ryan Lotz constructed this tribute to Lineage's Coolidge Corner neighborhood.

- ❖ 2 oz Sazerac 6 Year Rye
- ❖ 3/4 oz Punt e Mes
- ❖ 1/4+ oz Clear Creek Douglas Fir Eau de Vie
- ❖
- ❖ *Stir with ice and strain into a cocktail glass. Twist a lemon peel over the top.*

Copley Lady

Josh Taylor at Eastern Standard crafted this drink that was named for its similarity to the Creole Lady.

- ❖ 2 oz Sazerac 6 Year Rye
- ❖ 1/2 oz Barbeito Bual Boston Special Reserve Madeira
- ❖ 1/2 oz Amaro Nonino
- ❖ 1 dash Fee's Chocolate Bitters
- ❖
- ❖ *Stir with ice and strain into a rocks glass.*

Costa R.I.

An adaptation of a drink created at Highland Kitchen in honor of where Narragansett beer used to be brewed.

❖ 1 1/2 oz Lunazul Tequila
❖ 1 oz Grapefruit Juice
❖ 1/2 oz St. Germain

Shake with ice and strain into a salt-rimmed water goblet filled with fresh ice. Top with 2 oz Narragansett beer, garnish with a lime wedge, and add a straw.

Coup d'Etat

Josh Taylor's Scotch variation of the El Presidente at Eastern Standard.

❖ 1 1/2 oz Johnnie Walker Red Blended Scotch
❖ 3/4 oz Grenadine
❖ 1/2 oz Punt e Mes
❖ 1/4 oz Bauchant Orange Liqueur
❖ 1 barspoon Fernet Branca

Stir with ice and strain into a cocktail glass.

Costa R.I.,
Highland Kitchen

Cravat

Created by Brayden Burroughs, Esq., of Dudekicker for a Bols Genever industry event at the Franklin.

- 2 oz Bols Genever
- 1/2 oz Luxardo Amaretto
- 1/4 oz Lemon Juice
- 2 dash Angostura Bitters
- 1 dash Peychaud's Bitters

Stir with ice and strain into a rocks glass with fresh ice.

Creole Fizz

This Sazerac crossed with a Tiki drink hybrid was served at Drink for a Pernod Absinthe Bar Crawl.

- 1 1/2 oz Rittenhouse 100 Rye
- 1/2 oz Pineapple Juice
- 1/2 oz Orgeat
- 1/4 oz Pernod Absinthe
- 1/4 oz Peychaud's Bitters
- 1/2 Egg White

Shake without ice and then with ice. Strain into a Fizz glass, top with ~2 oz soda water, and add a straw. Grate cinnamon over the top.

Crocus

A No. 9 Park original that was inspired by the Chrysanthemum from the Savoy Cocktail Book.

- 1 1/2 oz Plymouth Gin
- 1 1/4 oz Noilly Prat Dry Vermouth
- 1/4 oz Kübler Absinthe
- 1/4 oz Crème de Violette
- 1/4 oz Bénédictine

Stir with ice and strain into a cocktail glass.

Crossing to Calais

Misty Kalkofen recalls crossing the English Channel with this Martinez variation.

- 1 3/4 oz Ransom Old Tom Gin
- 1 oz Bonal Gentiane-Quinquina
- 1/2 oz Cherry Heering
- 1 barspoon Combier Triple Sec

Stir with ice and strain into a cocktail glass. Garnish with a lemon twist.

Crush on a Bartender

Fred Yarm's tribute to the "Crush on a Stripper" shot series at Brick and Mortar.

1/2 oz Sombra Mezcal
1/2 oz Drambuie
1/2 oz Lime Juice

Shake with ice and strain into a shot glass rinsed with absinthe.

Cuban Anole

Ben Sandrof's Mai Tai variation that made its way on to the menu at Manhattan's PKNY bar.

1/2 oz Neisson Rhum Agricole Blanc
1/2 oz Appleton Reserve Rum
1/2 oz Plantation Barbados Rum
3/4 oz Lime Juice
1/2 oz Cinnamon Syrup
1/2 oz Orgeat

Shake with ice and strain into a rocks glass filled with crushed ice. Grate cinnamon over the top and add a straw.

Cucumber Fizz

Created by Will Thompson at Drink.

1 1/2 oz Hendrick's Gin
1/2 oz Cynar
1/2 oz Lemon Juice
1/2 oz Simple Syrup
1 Egg White
3 inch piece English Cucumber (no peel)
1 pinch Salt

Muddle cucumber with salt. Add rest of ingredients and shake; add ice and shake again. Double strain into a Highball glass containing 2 oz soda water. Garnish with a dash of celery bitters and add a straw.

Cynar Flip

With its sweet, spiritous, and bitter elements, Cynar is a cocktail in a bottle. Likewise, this simple but elegant Flip was conjured by Ben Sandrof and Corey Bunnewith at Drink.

❖ 2 1/2 oz Cynar
❖ 1 Whole Egg

Shake without ice and then with ice. Strain into a cocktail glass. Freshly grated nutmeg is sometimes added as a garnish.

Czech Julep

Created by Sean Frederick at the Citizen Public House in Boston.

❖ 2 oz Becherovka
❖ 1/2 oz Honey Syrup
❖ 1/2 oz Lemon Juice
❖ 1 barspoon Ardbeg Scotch
❖ 1 dash Bittermens Tiki Bitters

Shake with ice and strain into a Julep cup or Collins glass filled with crushed ice. Add a straw and garnish with mint sprigs and 2 dashes of Angostura Bitters.

Dancing Scotsman

An Air Mail-like tribute to Tommy Dewar at Eastern Standard.

❖ 1 oz Dewar's Scotch
❖ 1 oz Lemon Juice
❖ 1 oz Honey Syrup

Shake with ice and strain into a coupe. Fill with ~2 oz sparkling wine and garnish with a flamed lemon twist.

Daisy Black

Green Street's Dylan Black's homage to his great-grandfather who was a barman as well.

❖ 1 1/2 oz Old Overholt Rye
❖ 3/4 oz Lemon Juice
❖ 3/4 oz Honey Syrup

Shake with ice and strain into a cocktail glass. Garnish with a spanked mint leaf.

Dark Horse

A delicious Flip created by California Gold using a stout syrup that Drink had in house.

- 1 1/2 oz White Horse Scotch
- 3/4 oz Cynar
- 3/4 oz Guinness Syrup
- 2 dash Fee's Whiskey Barrel Bitters
- 1 Whole Egg

Shake without ice and then with ice. Strain into a coupe glass and garnish with grated nutmeg.

Darkside Iced Tea

Chad Arnholt, then of the Woodward and Citizen Public House, made this riff on the Long Island Iced Tea for a Fernet Branca industry event at the Franklin Southie.

- 1/2 oz Rittenhouse 100 Rye
- 1/2 oz Zaya Gran Reserva Rum
- 1/2 oz Fernet Branca
- 1/2 oz Combier Orange Liqueur
- 1/2 oz Lemon Juice
- 1/2 oz Simple Syrup

Shake with ice and pour unstrained into a Collins glass. Garnish with a lemon wedge and add a straw.

Dartmouth Highball

Bobby McCoy honors one of the Boston Tea Party ships at Eastern Standard cerca 2008.

- 1 1/2 oz Pimm's No. 1
- 3/4 oz Plymouth Gin
- 3/4 oz Lemon Juice
- 3/4 oz Simple Syrup
- 5-7 Mint Leaves

Shake with ice and double strain into a Highball glass filled with fresh ice. Top with Barritts Ginger Beer, garnish with mint, and add a straw.

Dead Man's Mule (variation)

Created by Drink bartenders John Gertsen and Joe Staropoli to fulfill a request for a recipe that normally calls for Goldschläger, a liqueur they do not carry.

- 1 oz Orgeat
- 1 oz Kübler Absinthe
- 1/2 oz St. Elizabeth Allspice Dram
- 1/2 of a Lime (in wedges)

Muddle lime wedges in the bottom of a copper mug. Add rest of ingredients, fill with crushed ice, and top with ginger beer. Add straws.

Death By Misadventure

Aaron Butler crafted this beer Highball at Russell House Tavern for the Sobieski tasting room at Tales of the Cocktail 2010.

❖ 2 oz Sobieski Vanilla Vodka
❖ 1 1/2 oz Meletti Amaro
❖ 3/4 oz Lemon Juice
❖ 3 dash Fee's Whiskey Barrel Bitters
❖ 3 dash Peychaud's Bitters
❖

❖ *Shake with ice and strain into a Collins glass filled with fresh ice cubes. Top with ~2 oz Rogue Dead Guy Ale, and add a straw.*

Defensio

Scott Holliday's rum variation of the Lucien Gaudin Cocktail at Rendezvous.

◆ 1 oz La Favorite Rhum Agricole Ambré
❖ 1/2 oz Cointreau
❖ 1/2 oz Campari
❖ 1/2 oz Noilly Prat Dry Vermouth
❖

❖ *Stir with ice and strain into a cocktail glass. Garnish with an orange twist.*

Dark Horse, Drink

Degüello

John Mayer at Craigie on Main named this drink after the song Santa Anna's troops played to the Americans trapped in the Alamo as part of a psych-ops campaign.

❖ 3/4 oz Scorpion Mezcal
❖ 3/4 oz Oloroso Sherry
❖ 3/4 oz Punt e Mes
❖ 1/2 oz Old Monk Rum
❖ 1/4 oz Simple Syrup
❖ 1 dash Angostura Bitters
❖ 5 drop Angostura Orange Bitters

❖ *Stir with ice and strain into a rocks glass. Garnish with a flamed orange twist.*

Déjà Vu in Dehli

A companion to Brother Cleve's Maharaja's Revenge on Green Street's menu.

❖ 2 oz Old Monk Rum
❖ 1/2 oz St. Germain
❖ 1/2 oz Lime Juice
❖ 2 dash Bittermens Tiki Bitters

❖ *Shake with ice and strain into a cocktail glass. Garnish with a lime wedge.*

Des Esseintes

Craigie on Main's John Mayer was moved by the eccentric protagonist of Joris-Karl Huysmans' A Rebours.

❖ 1 1/2 oz Del Maguey Chichicapa Mezcal
❖ 1 1/2 oz Amaro Nonino
❖ 1 barspoon Maraschino Liqueur
❖ 2 dash Angostura Bitters
❖ 2 dash Regan's Orange Bitters

❖ *Stir with ice and strain into a cocktail coupe. Garnish with an orange twist.*

Door 74

Deep Ellum's Max Toste was inspired by a drink he had at Door 74, a speakeasy in Amsterdam.

❖ 1 1/2 oz Laird's Applejack
❖ 3/8 oz Grenadine
❖ 1/2 oz Lemon Juice
❖ 1/2 oz Martini & Rossi Dry Vermouth
❖ 1 dash Orange Blossom Water
❖ 1 dash Peychaud's Bitters

❖ *Shake with ice and strain into a cocktail coupe. Garnish with an orange twist.*

Doubleplus-good

A white Mai Tai variant by Drink's John Gertsen that he crafted for a guest shift at the Edison in Los Angeles and named after a George Orwell reference.

❖
❖ 2 oz Matusalem Platino Rum
❖ 1 oz Lime Juice
❖ 1/2 oz Orgeat
❖ 1/2 oz Cointreau
❖ 1/2 Egg White
❖
❖ *Shake without ice and then with ice. Strain into a rocks glass and garnish with drops of Angostura bitters arranged in the shape of a pair of '+' symbols.*

Dover

Ryan Lotz thought up this absinthe-less Corpse Reviver #2 riff for a Gin & Tonic drinker at Lineage.

❖ 3/4 oz Berkshire Ethereal Gin
❖ 3/4 oz Lime Juice
❖ 3/4 oz Combier Orange Liqueur
❖ 3/4 oz Cocchi Americano
❖
❖ *Shake with ice and strain into a rocks glass. Fill with ice, add straws, and garnish with a lime wedge.*

Down at the Dinghy

Created by Rob Kraemer of Cambridge's Chez Henri for a J.D. Salinger-themed charity event at the Hawthorne.

❖ 2 oz Bushmills Irish Whiskey
❖ 1/2 oz Yellow Chartreuse
❖ 1/2 oz Cucumber Syrup
❖ 1/2 oz Lemon Juice
❖
❖ *Shake with ice and strain into a flute or cocktail glass.*

Dunaway

A tribute to Faye Dunaway that Misty Kalkofen crafted at Drink and submitted to the Vinos de Jerez Cocktail Competition in 2009.

❖ 2 1/4 oz. Lustau Fino Sherry
❖ 1/2 oz Cynar
❖ 1/2 oz Luxardo Maraschino Liqueur
❖ 2 dash Angostura Orange Bitters
❖
❖ *Stir with ice and strain into a cocktail glass. Garnish with a lemon twist.*

❖ Whiskey Smash,
❖ Eastern Standard

Dunbar

Drink bartender California Gold's riff on the Bobby Burns with naming help from poet Jill McDonough.

❖ 1 3/4 oz Douglas XO Scotch
❖ 1 oz Lustau Dry Amontillado
❖ Sherry
❖ 1/4 oz Bénédictine
❖ 1 dash Angostura Bitters
❖ 1 dash Angostura Orange Bitters

❖ *Stir with ice and strain into a coupe*
❖ *glass rinsed with Laphroaig Scotch.*
◆ *Twist an orange peel over the top.*

Dutch Masters

As a nod to the cherry liqueur or the tobacco brand, Scott Holiday mixed this brandy High Hat of sorts at Rendezvous in Cambridge.

❖ 2 1/4 oz Cognac
❖ 1 oz Cherry Heering
❖ 3/4 oz Lemon Juice
❖ 1 dash Angostura Bitters

❖ *Shake with ice and strain into a*
❖ *cocktail glass.*

Dwight Street Book Club

Created by Todd Maul at Clio.

- ❖ 2 oz El Dorado White Rum
- ❖ 1 oz Lemon Juice
- ❖ 1 oz Carpano Sweet Vermouth
- ❖ 1/2 oz Pedro Ximénez Sherry
- ❖ 1/2 oz Cinnamon Syrup
- ❖
- ❖ *Shake with ice and strain into a cocktail glass.*

◆

Earth Flipped

A Flip by Nicole Lebedevitch at Eastern Standard.

- ❖ 1 oz Lustau East India Solera Sherry
- ❖ 1 oz Brandy
- ❖ 1/2 oz Yellow Chartreuse
- ❖ 1/2 oz Cynar
- ❖ 2 dash Angostura Bitters
- ❖ 1 Whole Egg

- ❖ *Shake without ice and then with ice.*
- ❖ *Strain into a couple glass.*

◆

Eastern Standard's Whiskey Smash

Eastern Standard took this adaptation of an old drink to new levels by celebrating in 2009 the sale of 21,000 of them in their first 4 years!

- ❖ 2 oz W.L. Weller Bourbon
- ❖ 1 oz Simple Syrup
- ❖ 1/2 Lemon cut up into 4 pieces
- ❖ 4 Mint Leaves
- ❖
- ❖ *Muddle the lemon wedges and mint in a shaker. Add whiskey, syrup, and ice. Shake and double strain into a rocks glass filled with crushed ice. Garnish with fresh mint sprigs and add straws.*
- ❖

◆

Eighty Years War

Ryan Lotz's tribute to the Dutch War of Independence against Spain that he crafted at Lineage in Brookline.

- ❖ 1 1/2 oz Bols Genever
- ❖ 1 1/2 oz Lustau Dry Amontillado Sherry
- ❖ 1/8 oz Amer Picon (or Ramazzotti)
- ❖ 1/8 oz Bénédictine
- ❖ 1 pinch Salt

- ❖ *Stir with ice and strain into a rocks glass filled with fresh ice. Add straws.*

EL

El Brioso

The re-release of Crème Yvette inspired Drink's John Gertsen to riff on the Rosita.

❖ 1 1/2 oz Blanco Tequila
❖ 1/2 oz Crème Yvette
❖ 1/2 oz Campari
❖ 1/2 oz Dolin Blanc Vermouth
❖ 1 dash Angostura Bitters

❖ *Stir with ice and strain into a cocktail glass. Twist an orange peel over the top.*

◆

El Capitan

Jackson Cannon's take on a Pisco Manhattan. He used Eastern Standard's bitter brew (Cynar, Fernet, Creole Shrub) that served as their Amer Picon substitute.

❖ 1 oz Macchu Pisco
❖ 1 oz Carpano Sweet Vermouth
❖ 3/4 oz Cynar
❖ 1/4 oz Luxardo Fernet (or Fernet Branca)
❖ 1/8 oz Clément Creole Shrubb Orange Liqueur

❖ *Stir with ice and strain into a rocks glass. Garnish with an orange twist.*

◆

Elixir Alpestre

Eastern Standard's Bobby McCoy won the 2010 St. Germain Can-Can Classic with this libation.

❖ 2 oz Bols Genever
❖ 3/4 oz St. Germain
❖ 1/4 oz Becherovka
❖ 1 dash Angostura Orange Bitters
❖ 6 drop Pernod Absinthe

❖ *Stir with ice and strain into a coupe glass. Garnish with a lemon twist.*

◆

Elizabetta

Paul Manzelli's tribute to Elisabetta Nonino quickly became a popular menu item at Bergamot in Somerville.

❖ 1 1/2 oz Old Weller Antique Bourbon
❖ 1 oz Amaro Nonino
❖ 1/2 oz Cynar

❖ *Stir with ice and strain into a rocks glass. Garnish with a grapefruit twist.*

El Jimador Re-Animador

Adapted from a Corpse Reviver #2 riff created by Kathleen Semanski of Scholars Lounge in Boston for Saveur's Cointreau competition.

❖ 3/4 oz Reposado Tequila
❖ 3/4 oz Cointreau
❖ 3/4 oz Lillet Blanc
❖ 3/4 oz Lime Juice
❖ 1/4 oz Green Chartreuse

❖ Shake with ice and strain into a cocktail glass. Garnish with a lemon twist.

Emerald Toucan

Estragon's Sahil Mehta invented this Yellow Bird riff for the Galliano cocktail contest in 2012.

❖ 3/4 oz Tequila
❖ 3/4 oz Galliano
❖ 3/4 oz St. Germain
❖ 3/4 oz Lime Juice
❖ 1 dash Angostura Bitters

❖ Shake with ice and strain into a cocktail coupe. Garnish with a lime twist.

Emma Goldman

A LUPEC Boston original for a Women's Equality Day Celebration menu at the Franklin Southie. "If I can't drink, I don't want to be in your revolution."

❖ 2 oz Bols Genever
❖ 3/4 oz St. Germain
❖ 3/4 oz Carpano Sweet Vermouth
❖ 2 dash Angostura Bitters

❖ Stir with ice and strain into a rocks glass. Garnish with an orange twist.

ES Gin Flip

Eastern Standard's classic Flip that they hide away on the dessert menu.

❖ 2 oz Beefeater Gin
❖ 1/2 oz Orgeat
❖ 1 heaping barspoon Sugar
❖ 1 Whole Egg

❖ Shake without ice and then with ice. Strain into a coupe glass and garnish with freshly grated nutmeg.

Esmeralda

Created by Ben Sandrof then of
Drink using Armazem Viera's
Esmeralda Cachaça.

- 1 1/2 oz Cachaça
- 1/2 oz St. Germain
- 1/2 oz Lime Juice
- 1/2 oz Simple Syrup

Shake with ice and strain into a
coupe glass rinsed with a smokey
Scotch.

Esmino's Escape

Drink's Joe Staropoli was inspired
by Beach Bum Berry's tales about
the Esmino brothers during
wartime.

- 1 1/2 oz Batavia Arrack
- 1/2 oz Del Maguey Minero Mezcal
- 1/2 oz Angostura Bitters
- 1/2 oz Mathilde Orange Liqueur
- 1/4 oz Simple Syrup
- 1 barspoon Lemon Juice

Shake with ice and strain into a
rocks glass filled with crushed ice.
Garnish with a lime twist and a
cherry, and add a straw.

Espirit d'Escalier

An almost last word by Kevin
Martin at Eastern Standard.

- 3/4 oz Eagle Rare 10 Year Bourbon
- 3/4 oz Aperol
- 3/4 oz Pink Grapefruit Juice
- 3/4 oz Amaro Nonino

Shake with ice and strain into a
cocktail glass.

Essence of Winter Sleep

Scott Holliday was moved by
Robert Frost's "After Apple-Pick-
ing" poem at Rendezvous.

- 1 oz Laird's Applejack
- 1/4 oz Bénédictine
- 3-4 dashes Boker's (or Angostura) Bitters

Stir with ice and strain into a Champagne flute rimmed with sugar. Top
with ~3 oz Clos Normandy sparkling
cider.

Esmino's Escape, Drink

Everybody is a Nun

Created by Craigie on Main's Ted Gallagher for a J.D. Salinger-themed charity event held at the Hawthorne.

❖ 3/4 oz Willet Rye
❖ 1/2 oz Green Chartreuse
❖ 1/4 oz Yellow Chartreuse
❖ 1/2 oz Lime Juice
❖ 1/4 oz Lemon Juice
❖ 1/2 tsp Dry Lavender Flowers
❖ 2 dash Bittermens Boston Bittahs

Shake with ice and double strain into a Highball glass with ice. Add 2 oz dry sparkling wine, stir, and add a straw. Garnish with a lemon wheel rolled in dry lavender flowers.

Ewing No. 33

Dylan Black honored Patrick Ewing who grew up within blocks of Green Street in Cambridge.

❖ 2 oz Appleton VX Rum
❖ 1/2 oz Fernet Branca
❖ 1/4 oz Spiced Brown Sugar Syrup
❖ 1 dash Angostura Bitters

Stir with ice and strain into a coupe rinsed with pastis. Garnish with a lime wedge. Regular brown sugar syrup will substitute in a pinch.

71

Exhibition Swizzle

At Lineage, Ryan Lotz created this tribute to Aperol's introduction at the Padua Exhibition in 1919.

* 1 1/2 oz Barbancourt Rum
* 3/4 oz Lime Juice
* 1/2 oz Aperol
* 1/2 oz Velvet Falernum

Add ingredients to a tall glass, fill with crushed ice, and swizzle until cold. Garnish with 2 dashes of Tiki or Angostura Bitters, 2 mint sprigs, and a cherry, and add a straw.

Far East Suite

Bergamot's variation on the classic East India Cocktail.

* 1 1/2 oz Pierre Ferrand Cognac
* 1 1/2 oz Pineapple Juice
* 1/2 oz Combier Orange Liqueur
* 1 barspoon Batavia Arrack
* 1 dash Fee's Aromatic Bitters
* 2 Cloves

Muddle cloves in bitters. Add rest of ingredients and ice, shake, and double strain into a cocktail glass. Grate nutmeg over the top as a garnish.

Farley Mowat

Inspired by the Alaska Cocktail, this was created in part by John Gertsen at Drink and named after a famous environmentalist.

* 2 oz Anchor Distilling Junipero Gin
* 3/4 oz Boissiere Dry Vermouth
* 1/4 oz Herbsaint
* 6 drop Celery Bitters

Stir with ice and strain into a rocks glass. Twist a lemon peel over the top.

Farmhouse Flip

An adaptation of an Eastern Standard Flip that used walnut-infused Bourbon.

* 1 1/2 oz Bourbon
* 3/4 oz Lustau East India Solera Sherry
* 1/2 oz Maple Syrup
* 1/4 oz Walnut Liqueur
* 2 dash Angostura Bitters
* 1 Whole Egg

Shake without ice and then with ice. Strain into a cocktail coupe and garnish with freshly grated nutmeg.

Fears and Failures

One of Misty Kalkofen's beer cocktail for a Spin the Bottle event at Brick and Mortar featuring Chris Lohring of Notch Brewing.

❖ 1 oz Becherovka
❖ 1/2 oz Nux Alpina Walnut Liqueur
❖ 1/2 oz Lemon Juice
❖ 1/4 oz Honey Syrup

Shake with ice and strain into a rocks glass containing fresh ice. Top with ~2 1/2 oz Notch Saison beer and give a quick stir.

Fécamp 500

One of the menu items at a Franklin Southie Bénédictine industry event to celebrate the liqueur's half millennial anniversary.

❖ 2 oz Laird's Applejack
❖ 3/4 oz Bénédictine
❖ 1/2 oz Lemon Juice
❖ 1/2 oz Honey Syrup
❖ 2 dash Bitter Truth Lemon Bitters

Shake with ice and strain into a cocktail glass. Garnish with a lemon twist.

Fernet Buck

Deep Ellum of Allston's flavorful Highball.

❖ 1 1/2 oz Fernet Branca
❖ 1 oz Lime Juice
❖ 1 dash Angostura Bitters

Shake with ice and pour into a Highball glass. Top with ~3 oz AJ Stephans Ginger Beer and add a straw.

Fernet Pina Colada

Author's recreation of Hungry Mother's No. 34, a recipe that was lost except for the list of ingredients.

❖ 1 1/2 oz Spiced Rum
❖ 1/2 oz Fernet Branca
❖ 1 oz Coco Lopez Cream of Coconut
❖ 3 oz Pineapple Juice

Shake with ice and strain into a crushed iced-filled Tiki mug or Collins glass. Garnish with a paper umbrella and/or pineapple wedge and cherry. Add a straw.

Figawi

The Citizen Public House named their Daiquiri variation after an annual sailboat race from Hyannis to Nantucket. Where the figawi?

❖ 2 oz Banks Rum
❖ 3/4 oz Lime Juice
❖ 3/4 oz Five Spice Syrup

❖ *Shake with ice and strain into a rocks glass.*

◆

Final Voyage

A nautical Last Word created by Ryan Lotz and Brendan Pratt at Lineage.

❖ 3/4 oz Smith & Cross Rum
❖ 3/4 oz Rothman & Winter Apricot
   Liqueur
❖ 3/4 oz Green Chartreuse
❖ 3/4 oz Lime Juice

❖ *Shake with ice and strain into a cocktail glass.*

Fino Swizzle, Hawthorne

CRISTOPOLISTICARISTOPOLISTICARISTOPOLISTICARISTOPOLISTICARISTOPOLISTICARIS

Fin du Saison

A late Summer offering at Craigie on Main.

- ❖ 4 slice Small Cucumber
- ❖ 6-8 leaf Basil
- ❖ 1 pinch Salt
- ❖ 1 oz Cocchi Americano
- ❖ 1/2 oz Green Chartreuse
- ❖ 1/2 oz Lemon Juice
- ❖ 1/4 oz Grand Marnier

❖ *Muddle cucumber, basil leaves, and salt. Add rest of ingredients, shake with ice, and double strain into a Champagne flute. Top with a dry sparkling wine such as Veuve du Vernay.*

◆

Fino Swizzle

Nicole Lebedevitch found a way to use the extra syrup that came in the cans of cherries at the Hawthorne.

- ❖ 1/2 oz Pierre Ferrand 1840 Cognac
- ❖ 1/2 oz Graham's Ruby Port
- ❖ 3/4 oz Luxardo Cherry Jar Syrup
- ❖ 1/4 oz Lemon Juice
- ❖

❖ *Add the ingredients to a Collins glass filled with crushed ice. Swizzle until the glass is frosted. Float 2 oz Gutierrez Colosia Fino Elcano Sherry, garnish with 5 dashes Fee's Whiskey Barrel Bitters, and add a straw. If you do not have enough syrup from the cherry jar, supplement with Cherry Heering or other sweet cherry liqueur.*

◆

Fire in the Orchard

Apple, pear, and smoke at No. 9 Park.

- ❖ 1 1/4 oz Laird's Bonded Apple Brandy
- ❖ 1/4 oz Del Maguey Mezcal Vida
- ❖ 1/2 oz Belle de Brillet Pear Liqueur
- ❖ 3/4 oz Cocchi Americano
- ❖ 1/2 oz Lemon Juice
- ❖ 1/4 oz Agave Nectar
- ❖

❖ *Shake with ice and strain into a rocks glass.*

FL

Flapper Jane

A LUPEC Boston original invented for their Boston Tea Party event in 2007 held speakeasy style on a moored boat in Boston Harbor.

❖ 1 3/4 oz Dry Gin
❖ 3/4 oz Wu Wei Tea Syrup
❖ 1/2 oz Lemon Juice
❖ 1 dash Peychaud's Bitters

Shake with ice and strain into a cocktail glass.

Flip Royal

A floral and spiced Flip crafted by Eastern Standard's Jackson Cannon.

❖ 2 oz King's Ginger Liqueur
❖ 1 oz Rooibos Tea Syrup
❖ 1 dash Angostura Bitters
❖ 1 pinch Salt
❖ 1 Whole Egg

Shake without ice and then with ice, and strain into a rocks glass. Top with 2 oz soda water and garnish with a pinch or two of a grated cinnamon, nutmeg, and coffee spice mix.

Florentine Flip

Created by Tom Schlesinger-Guidelli at Craigie on Main.

❖ 1 oz Amaro Nonino
❖ 3/4 oz Bénédictine
❖ 1 oz Punt e Mes
❖ 1 dash Angostura Bitters
❖ 1 dash Orange Blossom Water
❖ 1 Whole Egg

Shake without ice and then with ice. Strain into a coupe glass and garnish with a spanked mint leaf.

Flowers for Murphy

Tom Schlesinger-Guidelli's offering for a Roaring Twenties event at the Boston Athenaeum in 2007.

❖ 1 1/2 oz Dry Gin
❖ 3/4 oz Simple Syrup
❖ 3/8 oz Lime Juice
❖ 3/8 oz Grapefruit Juice
❖ 1/4 oz Green Chartreuse

Shake with ice and strain into a Champagne flute. Top with ~1 oz dry sparkling wine and garnish with a spanked mint leaf.

Flying Headlock

Another stunning grappa drink at Brick and Mortar in Cambridge.

❖ 1 1/2 oz Nardini Grappa Bianca
❖ 1 oz Lustau Amontillado Sherry
❖ 1 oz Pierre Ferrand Dry Curaçao
❖ 1 dash Angostura Bitters

Stir with ice and strain into a rocks glass. Garnish with a lemon twist.

Foglie Noce

John Gertsen's contribution to a Roaring Twenties event at the Boston Athenaeum in 2007 that he later served at No. 9 Park.

❖ 2 1/2 oz Laird's Applejack
❖ 1 oz Nocino Walnut Liqueur
❖ 2 dash Fee's Whiskey Barrel Bitters

Stir with ice and strain into rocks glass. Twist an orange peel over the top.

Forgetful Elephant

Strong and tasting like peanuts, this elephant of a drink was crafted by Ted Kilpatrick at No. 9 Park.

❖ 2 1/4 oz Booker's Bourbon
❖ 3/4 oz Luxardo Amaro Abano
❖ 1/2 oz Orgeat
❖ 1 pinch Smoked Salt

Stir with ice and strain into a rocks glass.

Fort Point Cocktail

Created by John Gertsen at Drink as the bar's signature cocktail that is a nod to their neighborhood.

❖ 2 oz Old Overholt Rye
❖ 1/2 oz. Punt e Mes
❖ 1/4 oz. Bénédictine

Stir with ice and strain into a cocktail glass. Garnish with a brandied cherry.

Fort Washington Flip

Misty Kalkofen named her Flip at Green Street in 2007 after a nearby Revolutionary War fortification in Cambridgeport.

❖ 1 1/2 oz Laird's Applejack
❖ 3/4 oz Bénédictine
❖ 1/2 oz Maple Syrup
❖ 1 Whole Egg

Shake without ice and then with ice. Strain into a wine glass and garnish with freshly grated nutmeg.

Forty Virtues

Drink's California Gold crafted this homage to Armagnac for the French Spirits Soirée at the Astor Center in Manhattan in 2011.

- 1 1/2 oz Armagnac
- 1/2 oz Dolin Blanc Vermouth
- 1/2 oz Green Chartreuse
- 1/2 oz Bonal Gentiane-Quinquina
- 1 dash Orange Bitters

Stir with ice and strain into a cocktail glass.

Four Moors

Sahil Mehta's tribute to Sardinia at Estragon in Boston.

- 1 1/2 oz Lustau Dry Amontillado Sherry
- 1 oz B.G. Reynolds Orgeat
- 1/2 oz Mirto Liqueur

Stir with ice and strain into a coupe glass. Garnish with a lemon twist.

Fourth Voyage

No. 9 Park's homage to Columbus' fourth voyage to the New World that first landed in Martinique before exploring other parts of the Caribbean and Central America.

- 2 oz Neisson Rhum Agricole Blanc
- 3/4 oz Averna
- 1/4 oz Rothman & Winter Apricot Liqueur
- 1/4 oz Lemon Juice
- 1/8 oz Riga Black Balsam (sub Fernet Branca)

Shake with ice and strain into a cocktail glass.

Franklin Mortgage Co.

Bartenders at Deep Ellum were inspired by a trip to the Franklin Mortgage & Investment Company in Philadelphia.

- 1 oz Ron Diplomatico Rum
- 1 oz Santa Teresa Claro Rum
- 1/4 oz Cynar
- 1/8 oz Green Chartreuse
- 1/8 oz Maraschino Liqueur
- 1/8 oz Simple Syrup

Stir without ice and pour into a rocks glass rinsed with Ardbeg Scotch. Note: this is a room-temperature cocktail so use no ice.

Frank_O

Todd Maul's riff on the Frank Sullivan cocktail at Clio.

- ❖ 2 oz Frapin VS Cognac
- ❖ 1/2 oz Plantation Barbados Rum
- ❖ 1/2 oz Luxardo Triple Sec
- ❖ 1/2 oz Lillet Blanc
- ❖ 1/2 oz Lemon Juice
- ❖
- ❖ *Stir with ice and strain into a snifter glass with a sugared rim and an ice cube.*

◆

Fratelli Fizz

Influenced by the Sureau Fizz, Fred Yarm created this tribute to the Fratelli Branca distillery which makes the popular amaro.

- ❖ 2 oz Fernet Branca
- ❖ 1/2 oz Lemon Juice
- ❖ 1/2 oz Lime Juice
- ❖ 1 oz Cream
- ❖ 1 Egg White
- ❖
- ❖ *Shake without ice and then with ice. Strain into a Highball glass containing 2 oz of soda water. Garnish with a mint sprig and an orange twist, and add a straw.*

◆

Frank-O, Clio

Fritz

Ryan Lotz's adventurous equal parts tribute to the abstract expressionist artist Fritz Bultman at Lineage in Brookline.

- 3/4 oz Peychaud's Bitters
- 3/4 oz Maraschino Liqueur
- 3/4 oz Anchor Junipero Gin
- 3/4 oz Punt e Mes

Stir with ice and strain into a rocks glass. Garnish with an orange twist.

Frolic Fizz

Eric Cross' popular floral refresher at Stoddard's.

- 2 oz Privateer White Rum
- 3/4 oz Grapefruit Juice
- 3/4 oz Honey Syrup
- 1/4 oz Lemon Juice
- 1/4 oz Crème de Violette
- 1 Egg White

Shake without ice and then with ice. Strain into a Highball glass and top with 2 oz of soda water. Garnish with dry lavender flowers and add a straw.

Gail Collins

Brick and Mortar's Misty Kalkofen crafted this tall drink to honor the New York Times' op-ed columnist.

- 1 1/4 Del Maguey Mezcal Vida
- 3/4 oz Plymouth Sloe Gin
- 1/2 oz Maraschino Liqueur
- 1/2 oz Lemon Juice
- 1 dash Angostura Orange Bitters

Shake with ice and strain into a Collins glass filled with fresh ice cubes. Top with 2-3 oz soda water and gently stir. Garnish with a lemon twist and add a straw.

Germination

Created at Deep Ellum in Allston.

- 2 oz Gin
- 3/4 oz St. Germain
- 1/2 oz Lemon Juice
- 2 dash Orange Bitters

Shake with ice and strain into a rocks glass.

Gerty

An inverse Sazerac created by Fred Yarm in honor of John Gertsen who taught him a love of the New Orleans classic at No. 9 Park.

❖ 3/4 oz Rye Whiskey
❖ 3/4 oz Peychaud's Bitters
❖ 3/4 oz Herbsaint
❖ 3/4 oz Simple Syrup

Stir with ice and strain into a rocks glass. Twist a lemon peel over the top.

Golden Monarch

Sahil Mehta's spiced Margarita variation at Estragon.

❖ 1 1/2 oz Reposado Tequila
❖ 1/2 oz Domaine de Canton
❖ 1/2 oz B.G. Reynolds Passion Fruit Syrup
❖ 3/4 oz Lime Juice
❖ 1/4 oz St. Elizabeth Allspice Dram

Shake with ice and pour into a rocks glass. Garnish with a lime wedge and add straws.

Good John

Created at Citizen Public House in Boston.

❖ 2 oz Jameson Irish Whiskey
❖ 1/2 oz Carpano Sweet Vermouth
❖ 1/2 oz Lemon Juice
❖ 1/4 oz Maraschino Liqueur
❖ 2 dash Jerry Thomas Decanter Bitters

Shake with ice and strain into a cocktail glass. Garnish with a lemon twist.

Good Things Come

Drink's Jeff Grdinich's Irish whiskey cocktail that appeared in Beta Cocktails.

❖ 1 3/4 oz Redbreast Irish Whiskey
❖ 1/2 oz Pedro Ximénez Sherry
❖ 1/2 oz Fernet Branca
❖ 1/4 oz Yellow Chartreuse
❖ 1 dash Scrappy's Lavender Bitters

Stir with ice and strain into a cocktail glass.

Groovy Child,
Citizen Restaurant,
Worcester

Gory Guerrero

Using Misty Kalkofen's tip about how well tequila and Drambuie pair, Fred Yarm created this tribute to a Mexican pro-wrestler.

1 1/2 oz Reposado Tequila
1/2 oz Drambuie
1/2 oz Pineapple Juice
1/2 oz Dry Vermouth
1 dash Fee's Whiskey Barrel Bitters

Shake with ice and strain into a cocktail glass.

Grass Roots

A rich root beer-flavored rum drink on the Tikisms section of Eastern Standard's menu.

3/4 oz Sailor Jerry Spiced Rum
3/4 oz Root Liqueur
3/4 oz Maple Syrup
3/4 oz Lime Juice

Shake with ice and strain into a cocktail glass.

Great King Street

Jared Sadoian's Rob Roy variation he created at Craigie on Main.

❖ 3/4 oz Great King Street Scotch
❖ 3/4 oz Cardamaro
❖ 1/2 oz Punt e Mes
❖ 1/2 oz Maraschino Liqueur
❖ 1 barspoon Crème de Mûre
❖ 1 dash Mole Bitters

Stir with ice and strain into a rocks glass. Twist a lemon peel over the top.

◆

Green Ghost Fizz

Ryan Lotz's tall version of the 1937 classic, the Green Ghost, that he modified at Lineage.

❖ 1 1/2 oz Plymouth Gin
❖ 1 oz Green Chartreuse
❖ 3/4 oz Lime Juice

Shake with ice and strain into a Highball glass. Top with 2 oz soda water, add a straw, and garnish with a long, wide orange twist.

◆

Groovy Child

Dave Delaney of Worcester's Citizen Restaurant was inspired by Jerry Thomas' Barbados Punch and named his drink after a Bob Marley song lyric.

❖ 1 1/2 oz Hendrick's Gin
❖ 3/4 oz Noilly Prat Dry Vermouth
❖ 3/4 oz Lime Juice
❖ 2 heaping barspoon Guava Jelly
❖ 1 barspoon Simple Syrup

Shake with ice and double strain into a cocktail glass. Garnish with 3 dried juniper berries.

◆

Guelaguetza

Misty Kalkofen came up with this drink for a class she taught at Barbara Lynch's Stir and later put it on the menu at Brick and Mortar.

❖ 1 3/4 oz Del Maguey Crema Mezcal
❖ 1/2 oz Crème de Cacao
❖ 1/4 oz S. Maria al Monte Amaro
❖ 1/2 oz Lemon Juice

Shake with ice and strain into a rocks glass. Substitute 1 1/2 oz regular mezcal plus 1 tsp agave nectar for the Crema.

Gypsy

Created at Toro in the South End of Boston.

2 oz Death's Door Gin
3/4 oz Yellow Chartreuse
3/4 oz St. Germain
1 oz Lime Juice

Shake with ice and strain into a cocktail glass. Garnish with a lime wedge.

Hanging Curve

Aaron Butler generated this riff on the Floridita Daiquiri at Russell House Tavern in Cambridge.

1 1/2 oz Barbancourt 8 Year Rum
3/4 oz Lime Juice
1/2 oz Grapefruit Juice
1/2 oz Aperol
1/2 oz Velvet Falernum
1 barspoon Crème de Cassis

Shake with ice and strain into a cocktail glass.

Happy Fanny

Jamie Walsh modified the Modernista at Stoddard's and named it after how much it pleased Fanny, one of the bar regulars.

1 1/2 oz Gosling's Rum
1/2 oz Green Chartreuse
1/2 oz Lime Juice
1/4 oz Simple Syrup
1 barspoon Pernod Absinthe
2 dash Peychaud's Bitters

Shake with ice and strain into a Collins glass filled with fresh ice. Top off with ~2 oz soda water, garnish with a lime wedge, and add a straw.

Hasta Manzana

Fred Yarm's Vieux Carré variation that was published in The Mutineer Magazine.

1 oz Reposado Tequila
1 oz Calvados
1 oz Sweet Vermouth
1 barspoon Bénédictine
1 dash Mole Bitters

Stir with ice and strain into a cocktail glass.

Hau'Oli

Eastern Standard's Kevin Martin named his Tiki drink after the Hawaiian word for happiness and joy.

- 3/4 oz Old Port Rum
- 3/4 oz Lemon Hart 151 Rum
- 1 oz Orange Juice
- 1/2 oz Lime Juice
- 1/2 oz Bols Triple Sec
- 1/4 oz Orgeat

Shake with ice and strain into a rocks glass filled with crushed ice. Garnish with a lime wheel and mint sprigs, and add straws.

Hayride

A Flip by Fred Yarm influenced by Jerry Thomas' Stone Fence, a classic that appears on the Green Street menu.

- 1 1/2 oz Rye Whiskey
- 1 oz Apple Cider (non-fermented)
- 1/2 oz Bénédictine
- 1 dash Angostura Bitters
- 1 Whole Egg

Shake without ice and then with ice. Strain into a rocks glass and garnish with 7 drops of St. Elizabeth Allspice Dram and an apple slice.

Headkick

An adaptation of a Jeff Grdinich creation at Drink that bares a lot of similarity to the classic High Kick.

- 1 oz Willet Rye
- 1 oz Dolin Dry Vermouth
- 1/2 oz Yellow Chartreuse
- 1/2 oz Kümmel
- 1 dash Angostura Orange Bitters
- 1 dash Celery Bitters

Stir with ice and strain into a rocks glass. Twist a lemon peel over the top.

Healer

A delightful cure-all crafted at The Gallows in the South End of Boston.

- 1 oz Old Overholt Rye
- 1 oz Mead
- 1/2 oz Honey Syrup
- 1/2 oz Lemon Juice
- 1 dash Fee's Aromatic Bitters

Stir with ice and strain into a rocks glass. Garnish with an orange twist.

Heather in Queue

Jackson Cannon came up with this drink to satisfy an Eastern Standard regular's request for a Hoskins after the Amer Picon stock ran out.

- 1 1/2 oz Plymouth Gin
- 3/4 oz Martini & Rossi Bianco Vermouth
- 1/2 oz Bauchant Orange Liqueur
- 1/4 oz Fernet Branca

Stir with ice and strain into a cocktail glass. Garnish with a flamed lemon twist.

Helen the Pacific

Tiki fanatic Randy Wong modified the Hell in the Pacific and named it after his wife Helen; this adaptation was frequently served at Drink's Tiki Sundays.

- 3/4 oz Lemon Hart 80 Rum
- 3/4 oz Neisson Rhum Agricole
- 3/4 oz Lime Juice
- 1/2 oz Maraschino Liqueur
- 1/4 oz St. Elizabeth Allspice Dram
- 1/4 oz Velvet Falernum
- 1/4 oz Grenadine
- 1/4 oz Simple Syrup

Shake with ice and strain into a Tiki mug filled with crushed ice. Add a straw and garnish with a lime twist and a cherry.

Helsingor

John Gertsen adapted a No. 9 Park cocktail called the Copenhagen since they lacked the requisite Gamel Dansk at Drink.

- 1 3/4 oz Rittenhouse 100 Rye
- 3/4 oz Rothman & Winter Apricot Liqueur
- 1/2 oz Simple Syrup
- 1/2 oz Angostura Bitters

Stir with ice and strain into a cocktail glass.

Her Majesty's Pearl

Misty Kalkofen at Drink created a cocktail to match a Watiki 7 song title by request of band member Randy Wong.

- 1 1/2 oz Rhum Agricole Blanc
- 1/2 oz Pierre Ferrand Cognac
- 1/2 oz St. Germain
- 1/2 oz Lemon Juice
- 1/4 oz Simple Syrup
- 7 drop Rose Water

Stir with ice and strain into a coupe glass.

Helen the Pacific, Drink

Honey Bearer

Bergamot's Kai Gagnon was inspired by a funky late season honey batch.

1 1/2 oz Scarlet Ibis Rum
1/2 oz Honey Syrup
1/2 oz Yellow Chartreuse
1/2 oz Lime Juice

Shake with ice and strain into a cocktail glass.

Honey Fitz

Eastern Standard's Jackson Cannon created this tribute to politician John Francis 'Honey Fitz' Fitzgerald and served it at Tales of the Cocktail in 2010.

1 1/2 oz Zacapa 23 Year Rum
3/4 oz Honey Syrup
3/4 oz Grapefruit Juice
2 dash Peychaud's Bitters

Shake with ice and strain into a cocktail glass.

HO

Hong Kong Cocktail

Eastern Standard's Jackson Cannon presented his creation at the Diageo Happy Hour at Tales of the Cocktail in 2011.

* 1 1/2 oz Bulleit Rye
* 1 1/2 oz Cocchi Americano
* 3/4 oz Pimm's No. 1
* 1 dash Regan's Orange Bitters

Stir with ice and strain into a cocktail glass.

Honky and the Donkey

Patrick Sullivan contributed the name to Misty Kalkofen's recipe at Brick and Mortar.

* 1 oz Del Maguey Mezcal Vida
* 1 oz Lustau Dry Amontillado Sherry
* 1/2 oz Bénédictine
* 1/2 oz Cocchi Americano
* 1 dash Angostura Orange Bitters

Stir with ice and strain into a rocks glass.

Hornet's Nest

Created at Deep Ellum in Allston.

* 1 1/2 oz Old Overholt Rye
* 1/2 oz Cinzano Sweet Vermouth
* 3/4 oz Mead
* 1/4 oz Pineapple Syrup
* 2 dash Aromatic Bitters

Shake with ice and strain into a coupe glass. Garnish with a lemon twist.

Ho Tally

John Mayer at Craigie on Main flipped around Eastern Standard's Tally-ho!

* 2 oz Pimm's No. 1
* 1/2 oz Blackberry Syrup
* 1/2 oz Lemon Juice
* 1 barspoon St. Elizabeth Allspice Dram
* 1 dash Tiki Bitters
* 1 Whole Egg

Shake without ice and then with ice. Strain into a coupe glass.

Hotel Haute-Savoie

Misty Kalkofen riffed on the classic Lawhill while at Drink in Boston; adapted from Absinthe Cocktails.

❖ 2 oz Rye Whiskey
❖ 1 oz St. Germain
❖ 1/2 oz Dry Vermouth
❖ 1 barspoon Kübler Absinthe
❖ 1 dash Orange Bitters

Stir with ice and strain into a cocktail glass.

Hot Old Fashioned

Max Toste's Toddy format of the Old Fashioned at Deep Ellum in Allston.

❖ 1 Sugar Cube
❖ 1 Luxardo Maraschino Cherry
❖ 2 Orange Slices
❖ 2 dash Peychaud's Bitters
❖ 2 dash Angostura Bitters
❖ 2 oz Four Roses Bourbon
❖ 1 1/2 oz Boiling Hot Water

Warm a rocks glass with boiling water. Meanwhile, muddle the sugar cube, orange slices, cherry, and bitters in the bottom of a shaker tin. Add Bourbon and give the ingredients a quick shake. Empty the hot water from the rocks glass and fine strain into it. Top with the jigger of boiling water and give a quick stir.

Houdini

An air of mystery created by Kevin Martin at Eastern Standard in Boston.

❖ 1 1/2 oz Bols Genever
❖ 3/4 oz Cocchi Americano
❖ 3/4 oz Bénédictine

Stir with ice and strain into a cocktail glass. Garnish with a lemon twist.

Howlin' Ghost

Drink's California Gold placed 2nd with this drink in Appleton's mixology competition in 2010.

❖ 2 oz Appleton Estate Reserve Rum
❖ 1/2 oz Punt e Mes
❖ 1/2 oz Simple Syrup
❖ 1/8 oz Lime Juice

Stir with ice and strain into a rocks glass. Garnish with lime and grapefruit twists and float a 1/4 oz of Kübler Absinthe.

Hugo Ball

For a Grand Marnier event at Drink, Matthew Schrage then of No. 9 Park paid tribute to the famous Dada artist.

❖ 1 1/2 oz Beefeater Gin
❖ 3/4 oz Grand Marnier
❖ 3/4 oz Cynar

❖ *Stir with ice and strain into a cock-*
❖ *tail glass. Garnish with an orange*
❖ *twist.*

Imperial Royale

LUPEC Boston's own Kirsten Amann and Joy Richard invented this surprisingly refreshing Highball.

❖ 1 1/2 oz St. Germain
❖ 12 oz can/bottle Bud Light Lime

❖ *Build in a pint glass with ice. Stir*
❖ *gently to combine and add a straw.*
❖ *Optional: garnish with a fresh rasp-*
❖ *berry.*

Indian Summer Julep,
Eastern Standard

Indian Summer Julep

A house original Autumn Julep that seasonally appears on the Eastern Standard menu.

1 oz Calvados
1 oz Old Monk Rum
1/2 oz Cinnamon Syrup
1 barspoon St. Elizabeth Allspice Dram
2 sprig Mint

Muddle the mint in a rocks glass. Add rest of the ingredients and fill with crushed ice. Garnish with fresh mint sprigs and grated nutmeg, and add straws.

Irish Coffee Fizz

Created by Misty Kalkofen at Drink for a Bushmills' St. Patrick's Day cocktail promotion.

3/4 oz Bushmills Irish Whiskey
1/2 oz Dark Rum
1/4 oz Navan Vanilla Liqueur
1/2 oz Simple Syrup
1/2 oz Cream
1 Egg White
8 Coffee beans

Muddle coffee beans in a shaker. Add rest of ingredients, and shake without ice and then with ice. Double strain into a Fizz or rocks glass containing 1 oz of soda water.

Irish Wolfhound

Created by Drink's Josey Packard and adapted from LUPEC Boston's Little Black Book of Cocktails.

1 1/2 oz Irish Whiskey
1/2 oz Grapefruit Juice
1/4 oz Lemon Juice
1/4 oz Maraschino Liqueur
3 drop Rose Water

Shake with ice and strain into a cocktail glass. Garnish with a grapefruit twist.

Irma la Douce

An original by LUPEC Boston for a Chartreuse event held at Green Street in 2007; the drink was named after the movie where Shirley MacClaine's character wore green stockings.

1 1/2 oz Hendrick's Gin
1/2 oz Green Chartreuse
1/2 oz Cucumber Juice
1/2 oz Lemon Juice
1/2 oz Grapefruit Juice
1/4 oz Simple Syrup

Shake with ice and strain into a cocktail glass. A cucumber wheel garnish would do no harm here.

Islay Louisiane

Ted Kilpatrick made this smokey variation of the De La Louisiane cocktail at No. 9 Park.

1 oz Talisker 10 Year Scotch
1 oz Bénédictine
1 oz Cocchi Sweet Vermouth
1/8 oz Kübler Absinthe
2 dash Peychaud's Bitters
2 dash Jerry Thomas Decanter Bitters

Stir with ice and strain into a rocks glass rinsed with Herbsaint. Twist a lemon peel over the top.

It's Like a Relationship

For Valentine's Day in 2012, this cocktail by Misty Kalkofen was included in a short list of bitter drinks at Brick and Mortar.

1 1/4 oz Nardini Grappa Bianca
1 1/4 oz Cynar
1/2 oz Combier Orange Liqueur
2 dash Angostura Bitters

Stir with ice and strain into a rocks glass.

Jaguar

Created by Tom Schlesinger-Guidelli at Eastern Standard.

1 1/2 oz Blanco Tequila
3/4 oz Green Chartreuse
3/4 oz Amer Picon
3 dash Orange Bitters

Stir with ice and strain into a cocktail glass. Garnish with a flamed orange twist.

Jalisco Buck

An herbal refresher from Berg-amot in Somerville.

1 oz Corralejo Tequila
1/2 oz Root Liqueur
1/2 oz Yellow Chartreuse
3/4 oz Lime Juice
1/4 oz Simple Syrup

Shake with ice and strain into a Highball glass filled with fresh ice. Top with 2 oz ginger beer, garnish with grated nutmeg, and add a straw.

Jamaican Bobsled

A house original for Drink's weekly Tiki Sunday nights.

3/4 oz Smith & Cross Rum
3/4 oz Wray & Nephew Overproof White Rum
1/2 oz Crème de Cacao
1/2 oz St. Elizabeth Allspice Dram
1/2 oz Ginger Syrup
2 dash Bittermens Mole Bitters

Shake with ice and strain into a Tiki mug filled with crushed ice. Top with extra crushed ice, add a straw, and garnish with a few dashes of Fee's Whiskey Barrel Bitters.

Jerez Flip

Created at Craigie on Main in Cambridge.

1 1/2 oz Dry Oloroso Sherry
3/4 oz Pimm's No. 1
3/4 oz Bénédictine
1/4 oz Brown Sugar Syrup
1 dash Angostura Bitters
1 dash Bittermens Mole Bitters
1 Whole Egg

Shake without ice and then with ice. Strain into a coupe glass and garnish with freshly grated nutmeg.

Jimador Sour

Bartenders at Craigie on Main were inspired by the release of the Galliano reformulation.

❖ 1 1/2 oz Siembra Azul Tequila
❖ 3/4 oz Lime Juice
❖ 3/4 oz Green Chartreuse
❖ 1/4 oz Galliano
❖ 1 dash Bittermens Tiki Bitters

Shake with ice and strain into a rocks glass with ice cubes.

Jimmy Lane Swizzle

An impromptu Swizzle crafted by Jimmy Lane at Eastern Standard.

❖ 1 1/2 oz Barbancourt 8 Year Rum
❖ 3/4 oz Spiced Syrup
❖ 3/8 oz Lemon Juice
❖ 3/8 oz Lime Juice
❖ 1 barspoon St. Elizabeth Allspice Dram

Muddle 2 mint sprigs at the bottom of a Highball glass. Add rest of ingredients and crushed ice, and swizzle but keeping the muddled mint at the bottom. Top with 2 dashes each of Angostura, Peychaud's, and orange bitters, garnish with fresh mint sprigs, and add a straw.

Joe Bans You

Todd Maul of Clio paid tribute to a customer's story about banning an overly inquisitive patron from his liquor store.

❖ 2 oz Soberano Spanish Brandy
❖ 1 oz Lime Juice
❖ 3/4 oz Sangre y Trabajadero Oloroso Sherry
❖ 1/2 oz Orgeat

Shake with ice and strain into a cocktail glass.

Joe's Fashion

For a James Beard event in 2007, Misty Kalkofen named her drink after a filly that Joseph Laird rode in the 1840s.

❖ 1 oz Gin
❖ 1 oz Laird's Applejack
❖ 1/2 oz Punt e Mes
❖ 1/2 oz Lemon Juice
❖ 1/2 oz Five Spice Syrup

Shake with ice and strain into a cocktail glass. Garnish with a lemon twist.

Johann Goes to Mexico

Drink's Josey Packard imagined if Angostura Bitters founder Dr. Johann Siegert traveled north from Venezuela.

❖ 1 1/2 oz Del Maguey Mezcal Vida
❖ 1/2 oz Angostura Bitters
❖ 1/2 oz Lemon Juice
❖ 1/2 oz Simple Syrup

❖ *Shake with ice and strain into a cocktail glass.*

Johnny Jump Up

Rendezvous' Scott Holliday paid tribute to Spring and Johnny Appleseed with this drink based off of the Corpse Reviver.

❖ 3/4 oz Morin Selection Calvados
❖ 3/4 oz Luxardo Triple Sec
❖ 3/4 oz Cocchi Americano
❖ 3/4 oz Lemon Juice
❖ 1 barspoon Pastis

❖ *Shake with ice and strain into a cocktail glass.*

Johnny Jump Up, Rendezvous

Journey Through the Night

Created by Kyle Powell at Russell House Tavern.

- 2 oz Tru Organic Gin
- 1 1/4 oz Plymouth Sloe Gin
- 1/4 oz Maraschino Liqueur
- 1/2 oz Lime Juice

Shake with ice and strain into a cocktail glass.

Jubilee Line

This "breakfast in Kennington" was served at Craigie on Main.

- 1 1/2 oz Beefeater Gin
- 1 Tbsp Seville Orange Marmalade
- 3/4 oz Triple Sec
- 3/4 oz Lemon Juice

Shake with ice and double strain into a cocktail glass.

Jupiter's Acorn

A nut fit for a god at Craigie on Main in Cambridge.

- 1 oz Barbancourt 15 Year Rum
- 1 oz Nux Alpina Walnut Liqueur
- 1/2 oz Punt e Mes
- 1/2 oz Bénédictine
- 1 Whole Egg
- 1 dash Angostura Bitters
- 1 dash Bittermens Mole Bitters

Shake without ice and then with ice. Strain into a coupe glass and garnish with freshly grated nutmeg.

J.R.T.

Created by Todd Maul and Randy Wong at Clio in Boston.

- 2 oz Ron Diplomático Reserve Rum
- 1 oz Lime Juice
- 1/2 oz St. Elizabeth Allspice Dram
- 1/2 oz Cinnamon Syrup

Shake with ice and strain into a rocks glass containing one large ice cube. Freshly grate nutmeg over the top of the drink and add a pinch or two of ground mace to the top of the ice cube. Add a straw.

Juan Bautista

Jared Sadoian at Craigie on Main named his drink after an Italian 16th century sailor and explorer hired by Spain to explore Peru.

- 1 oz Macchu Pisco
- 1 oz Aperol
- 1/2 oz Cynar
- 1/2 oz Lustau Dry Oloroso Sherry
- 2 dash Fee's Whiskey Barrel Bitters

Stir with ice and strain into a rocks glass filled with fresh ice. Garnish with an orange twist.

Justified Shooting

John Mayer's tribute to the Elmore Leonard television series at Local 149 in South Boston.

- 1 1/2 oz Balvenie Caribbean Cask Scotch
- 1 oz Amaro Nonino
- 1/2 oz Cynar
- 2 dash Bittermens Mole Bitters

Stir with ice and strain into a rocks glass.

Keep the Doctor Away

Sam Treadway at Drink used Hungry Mother's No. 47 as inspiration.

- 1 oz Rittenhouse 100 Rye
- 1 oz Laird's 7 1/2 Year Apple Brandy
- 1 oz Aperol
- 1/6 Gala Apple

Slice up the apple wedge into a dozen pieces. Add rest of ingredients and shake hard with ice to muddle up the apple. Double strain into a coupe glass and garnish with an apple slice.

Ken–Tiki

A LUPEC Boston original served at their 1950s-inspired Tiki Bash in 2009.

- 1 1/2 oz Eagle Rare Bourbon
- 3/4 oz Falernum
- 1/2 oz Campari
- 1/2 oz Passion Fruit Juice
- 1/2 oz Lemon Juice

Shake with ice and strain into a cocktail glass rinsed with Herbsaint.

Khartoum,
Brick and Mortar

Kentucky Royale

Created for a Buffalo Trace and Eagle Rare industry event at the Franklin Southie.

1 1/2 oz Eagle Rare Bourbon
1/2 oz Cherry Heering
1/2 oz Carpano Sweet Vermouth
1 barspoon Luxardo Espresso Liqueur
2 dash Bittermens Mole Bitters

Stir with ice and strain into a cocktail glass. Garnish with a brandied cherry.

Kentucky Werewolf

A tall, refreshing herbal libation at No. 9 Park.

1 oz Booker's Bourbon
3/4 oz Luxardo Limoncello
3/4 oz Yellow Chartreuse
1 dash Celery Bitters

Stir with ice and strain into a Highball glass containing fresh ice. Top with Fentimans tonic water. Garnish with a lemon twist and add a straw.

Khartoum

*Created by Misty Kalkofen of
Brick and Mortar in Cambridge.*

- 1 oz Cardamaro
- 1 oz Amaro Montenegro
- 1/2 oz Smith & Cross Rum

*Build in an ice-filled Collins glass
and garnish with a long Horse's
Neck-style orange peel. Top with
~2 oz soda water, gently stir, and
add a straw.*

King Caesar

*Island Creek Oyster Bar's tribute
to an 18th century Duxbury mer-
chant.*

- 3/4 oz Amaro Montenegro
- 3/4 oz Pineapple Juice
- 3/4 oz Lime Juice
- 1/2 oz Simple Syrup
- 1 dash Bittermens Tiki Bitters

*Shake with ice and strain into a
Champagne flute. Top with ~2 oz
Dibon Cava.*

King's Bitter

*Created at Island Creek Oyster
Bar in Boston.*

- 1 oz Maurin Quina
- 1/2 oz King's Ginger Liqueur
- 1/2 oz Carpano Sweet Vermouth
- 1/2 oz S. Maria al Monte Amaro
- 1/2 oz Lime Juice

*Shake with ice and strain into a
Champagne flute. Top with ~2 oz
prosecco.*

Kingston Fizz

*Influenced by a discussion at No.
9 Park about the Cuba Libre, Fred
Yarm made up his own Rum and
Coke variation.*

- 1 1/2 oz Aged Jamaican Rum
- 3/4 oz Lime Juice
- 1/2 oz St. Elizabeth Allspice Dram
- 1/4 oz Pernod
- 2 dash Angostura Bitters
- 1 Egg White

*Shake without ice and then with ice.
Add 2 oz of Coca Cola to a Fizz or
Highball glass, strain shaker's con-
tents over the top, and add a straw.*

King's Yellow

An Eastern Standard original with a resemblance to the classic Caprice.

❖ 1 1/2 oz Bombay Sapphire Gin
❖ 3/4 oz Dry Vermouth
❖ 3/4 oz Bénédictine
❖ 1 dash Orange Bitters

❖ *Stir with ice and strain into a cocktail glass rinsed with apricot liqueur. Garnish with a lemon twist.*

Kobayashi Maru

Soon after the 2011 earthquake in Japan, Aaron Butler at Russell House Tavern reached for the Japanese whisky and named the drink after a Star Trek reference for a no-win situation.

❖ 2 1/4 oz Yamazaki 12 Year Whisky
❖ 3/4 oz Green Tea Syrup
❖ 3/4 oz Lemon Juice
❖ 1/4 oz Apricot Liqueur
❖ 2 dash Angostura Orange Bitters
❖ 3 drop Orange Blossom Water

❖ *Shake with ice and strain into a cocktail glass.*

Kolb's Gem

Misty Kalkofen's popular seasonal sparkler at Green Street that she crafted for a Boston Magazine article.

❖ 3/4 oz Yellow Chartreuse
❖ 1/2 oz Lemon Juice
❖ 1 chunk Watermelon (~1 oz)

❖ *Shake with ice and double strain into a wine glass. Top off with ~3 oz of Brut Dargent Blanc de Blanc sparkling wine and garnish with a spanked mint leaf.*

Kuromatsu

Created by Drink's Will Thompson using the classic Japanese Cocktail as a starting point.

❖ 1 1/2 oz Cognac
❖ 3/4 oz Cynar
❖ 1/2 oz Zirbenz Stone Pine Liqueur
❖ 1/4 oz Monin Orgeat

❖ *Stir with ice and strain into a cocktail glass.*

Kysely

Eastern Standard's spiced Czech remake of a Pisco Sour.

1 1/2 oz Becherovka
3/4 oz Lemon Juice
3/4 oz Spiced Syrup
1 Egg White

Shake without ice and then with ice. Strain into a rocks glass and garnish with a dozen drops of Fee's Whiskey Barrel Bitters.

La Flora Vieja

Created by Tom Schlesinger-Guidelli at Eastern Standard and adapted from Green Street's cocktail book.

2 oz Blanco Tequila
1/2 oz St. Germain
1/4 oz Maraschino Liqueur
1 dash Angostura Bitters

Stir with ice and strain into a cocktail glass. Garnish with a flamed orange twist.

Lamplighter

A popular Sour at Chez Henri in Cambridge.

2 oz Bourbon
3/4 oz Celery Juice
1/4 oz Lemon Juice
1 oz Simple Syrup

Shake with ice and strain into a cocktail glass. Garnish with a lemon twist.

La Palabra

Ted Kilpatrick's mezcal take on the Last Word at No. 9 Park.

1 oz Del Maguey Mezcal Vida
1 oz Combier Triple Sec
1 1/4 oz Green Chartreuse
3/4 oz Lime Juice

Shake with ice and strain into a rocks glass.

LA

Lasky Last Knight

David Embury disciple Todd Maul riffed on the Knight from The Fine Art of Mixing Drinks at Clio.

- 2 oz Frapin VS Cognac
- 1 oz Lemon Juice
- 1/2 oz Luxardo Triple Sec
- 1/2 oz Green Chartreuse
- 1 dash Simple Syrup
- 1 dash Lemon Bitters

Shake with ice and strain into a cocktail glass. Garnish with a lemon twist.

Last Date

A tribute to dating life that Chad Arnholt at the Citizen Public House had a hand in creating.

- 1 oz Pierre Ferrand 1840 Cognac
- 1 oz Averna
- 1/2 oz Orgeat
- 1/2 oz Lemon Juice

Shake with ice and strain into rocks glass.

Last Letter

Adapted from a recipe by Evan Harrison of Brick and Mortar.

- 2 oz Reposado Tequila
- 1/2 oz Drambuie
- 1/2 oz Averna
- 2 dash Bittermens Mole Bitters

Stir with ice and strain into a rocks glass. Garnish with a lemon twist.

Latest Buzz

Stephen Shellenberger crafted this drink at Pomodoro in Brookline to showcase Brandymel honey liqueur.

- 3/4 oz Grappa di Moscato
- 3/4 oz Cristinalda Brandymel Honey Liqueur
- 3/4 oz Vergano Americano Chinato
- 3/4 oz Lime Juice

Shake with ice and strain into a wine glass.

Latest Word

Craigie on Main's malty update to the Last Word.

- 3/4 oz Bols Genever
- 3/4 oz Maraschino Liqueur
- 3/4 oz Green Chartreuse
- 3/4 oz Lime Juice

Shake with ice and strain into a cocktail glass. Garnish with a brandied cherry.

Latest Word,
Craigie on Main

Laura Lee

Todd Maul's variation of the High Hat that he created at Rialto in Cambridge and later served at Clio in Boston.

❖ 2 oz Old Overholt Rye
❖ 3/4 oz Rothman & Winter Apricot Liqueur
❖ 1/2 oz Lemon Juice
❖ 1/4 oz Cherry Heering
❖ 1 dash Fee's Whiskey Barrel Bitters

❖ *Stir with ice and strain into a coupe glass.*

Le Grande Flip

Described as Jackson Cannon's alcoholic Orange Julius, this Flip was created at Eastern Standard in Boston.

❖ 1 oz Laird's Applejack
❖ 1/2 oz Bénédictine
❖ 1/2 oz Orange Juice
❖ 1/2 oz Diabolique (infused Bourbon)
❖ 2 heaping barspoon Sugar
❖ 1 Whole Egg

❖ *Shake without ice and then with ice. Strain into a wine glass and garnish with an orange twist.*

Le Vieux Italian

A drink crafted by Aaron Butler at Russell House Tavern for a Pernod Absinthe bar crawl in 2010.

- 2 oz Pierre Ferrand Ambre Cognac
- 1 1/2 oz Averna
- 1/2 oz Pernod Absinthe
- 2 dash Fee's Whiskey Barrel Bitters

Stir with ice and strain into a rocks glass. Twist an orange peel over the top.

Le Quebecois

Kai Gagnon's north of the border concoction at Bergamot was inspired by the Brooklyn and Red Hook.

- 1 1/2 oz Old Overholt Rye
- 1/2 oz Dolin Dry Vermouth
- 1/2 oz Punt e Mes
- 1/2 oz Maraschino Liqueur
- 1 dash Bitter Truth Orange Bitters

Stir with ice and strain into a rocks glass. Garnish with a flamed orange twist.

Leonora Banks

Scott Mashall invented this riff of the Mary Pickford at Drink for the Banks Rum release party in 2010.

- 1 1/2 oz Banks Rum
- 1 oz Pineapple Juice
- 1/4 oz Maraschino Liqueur
- 1/4 oz Cinnamon Syrup
- 2 dash Bittermens Tiki Bitters

Shake with ice and strain into a Tiki mug filled with crushed ice. Garnish with freshly grated nutmeg and add a straw.

Les Champs Verts

An herbal charmer at Bergamot in Somerville that appears on the menu at the beginning of Summer each year.

- 1 oz Dolin Dry Vermouth
- 1 oz Dolin Blanc Vermouth
- 1/2 oz Green Chartreuse
- 1 fistful Anise Hyssop Leaves

Muddle leaves in other ingredients. Add ice, shake, and double strain into a Champagne flute. Top with sparkling wine. Rub the glass' rim with a smacked anise hyssop leaf.

Libretto

Created by John Mayer at Craigie on Main in Cambridge for a regular who was a librarian; the name stuck despite his realization that he had chosen the wrong Italian word.

❖ 1 1/2 oz Siete Leguas Añejo Tequila
❖ 3/4 oz Carpano Sweet Vermouth
❖ 1/2 oz St. Germain
❖ 1/2 oz Cynar
❖ 2 dash Mole Bitters

Stir with ice and strain into a rocks glass.

Lido Shuffle

Evan Harrison came up with this lower proof drink at Allston's Deep Ellum, and it later appeared on Brick and Mortar's menu after he started working there.

❖ 1 oz Cocchi Americano
❖ 1/2 oz Aperol
❖ 1/2 oz Yellow Chartreuse
❖ 1/2 oz Lemon Juice

Shake with ice and strain into a Highball glass filled with fresh ice. Top with ~2 oz soda water, garnish with an orange twist, and add a straw.

Lioness (of Brittany)

Created by Andrea Desrosiers and Frederic Yarm for a Grand Marnier event held at Drink in 2009, and named after an infamous 14th century female pirate.

❖ 1 1/4 oz Amber Rum
❖ 3/4 oz Grand Marnier
❖ 3/4 oz Darjeeling Tea (Cooled)
❖ 1/4 oz Lemon Juice

Stir with ice and strain into a cocktail glass rinsed with absinthe. Garnish with a lemon twist.

Little Otik

Alex Homans at Temple Bar paired the piquant Ransom gin with a spiced Czech liqueur.

❖ 2 oz Ransom Old Tom Gin
❖ 1/2 oz Becherovka
❖ 1/2 oz Cocchi Americano
❖ 1 dash Orange Bitters

Stir with ice and strain into a rocks glass. Garnish with a lemon twist.

LI-LO

Lizzie Asher

A floral Silver Fizz by Ryan Lotz at Lineage.

❖ 2 oz Macchu Pisco
❖ 1 oz Lemon Juice
❖ 1/2 oz Apricot Liqueur
❖ 1/2 oz Crème Yvette
❖ 1 Egg White

Shake without ice and then with ice. Strain into a Highball glass and top with ~2 oz of ginger beer. Twist an orange peel over the top and add a straw.

Loose Translation

Carrie Cole then of Craigie on Main presented this drink at the Bartenders on the Rise event at Green Street in 2010.

❖ 1 1/4 oz Scorpion Mezcal
❖ 3/4 oz Aperol
❖ 1/2 oz Mathilde Orange Liqueur
❖ 1/2 oz Pineapple Syrup
❖ 1/2 oz Lime Juice
❖ 1 dash St. Elizabeth Allspice Dram
❖ 1 dash Angostura Orange Bitters

Shake with ice and strain into a rocks glass with fresh ice. Top with 1 oz ginger ale. Garnish with a lime wedge and add a straw.

Mad Monk Fizz, No. 9 Park

Low Rider

One of Misty Kalkofen's early menu items at Brick and Mortar.

- ❖ 2 oz Siembra Azul Blanco Tequila
- ❖ 1/2 oz Zucca Rabarbaro Amaro
- ❖ 1/2 oz Crème de Cacao
- ❖ 1 dash Angostura Bitters
- ❖

❖ *Stir with ice and strain into a rocks*
❖ *glass.*

Mad Monk Fizz

No. 9 Park's Ted Kilpatrick was inspired by the Russian mystic Rasputin.

- ❖ 1 oz Zirbenz Stone Pine Liqueur
- ❖ 1 oz Fighting Cock Bourbon
- ❖ 1 oz Old Monk Rum
- ❖ 1/2 oz Vanilla Syrup
- ❖ 1 Whole Egg

❖ *Shake without ice and then with ice.*
❖ *Strain into a Highball glass contain-*
❖ *ing ~2 oz Old Rasputin Imperial*
❖ *Stout. Garnish with freshly ground*
❖ *pink peppercorns and add a straw.*

Maikai Mule

Kai Gagnon's Mule at Bergamot got named due to its similarities to the Mai Tai.

- ❖ 1 oz Matusalem Gran Reserva Rum
- ❖ 1/2 oz Becherovka
- ❖ 1/2 oz Pineapple Syrup
- ❖ 1/2 oz Orgeat
- ❖ 1/2 oz Lime Juice
- ❖

❖ *Shake with ice and strain into a*
❖ *copper mug (or rocks glass) filled*
❖ *with crushed ice. Top with ~1 oz*
❖ *ginger beer, garnish with mint, and*
❖ *add a straw.*

Magic Wand Malfunction

John Mayer at Craigie on Main lived up to his OnTheBar bio of "If the drink is named after Texas, firearms, or sex toys, there's a good chance I created it."

- ❖ 1 oz Citadel Reserve Gin
- ❖ 1 oz Becherovka
- ❖ 1/2 oz Lemon Juice
- ❖ 1/2 oz Maple Sugar Syrup
- ❖ 2 dash Jerry Thomas Decanter Bitters
- ❖

❖ *Shake with ice and strain into a*
❖ *coupe glass. Garnish with an orange*
❖ *twist. Note: maple sugar syrup*
differs from maple syrup.

Maharaja's Revenge

A Brother Cleve recipe that appears on the Green Street menu.

2 oz Old Monk Rum
1 oz Apricot Liqueur
3/4 oz Lime Juice

Shake with ice and strain into a cocktail glass. Garnish with a lime wheel.

Maldenado

Eastern Standard's tribute to one of their favorite barbacks.

1 oz Milagro Blanco Tequila
1/2 oz Agave Nectar
1/2 oz Lime Juice
1 dash Tabasco Sauce

Shake with ice and pour into a stemmed water glass. Top off with 4-5 oz Negro Modelo Beer and garnish with a lime wedge.

Manhattan Exposition

An abstract Manhattan variation by Jennifer Salucci at Deep Ellum.

2 oz Pierre Ferrand Ambre Cognac
1/2 oz Plymouth Sloe Gin
1/2 oz Dry Vermouth
2 dash Mole Bitters

Stir with ice and strain into a rocks glass. Twist a lemon peel over the top.

Maximilian Affair

Misty Kalkofen at Green Street invented this drink for Ron Cooper of Del Maguey who was a guest at her bar that night.

1 oz Mezcal
1 oz St. Germain
1/2 oz Punt e Mes
1/2 oz Lemon Juice

Shake with ice and strain into a cocktail glass.

Man With No Name

Deep Ellum's Tequila Sazerac variation.

- 2 oz Zapopan Blanco Tequila
- 1/4 oz Agave Nectar
- 5 dash Peychaud's Bitters
- 2 dash Mole Bitters

Stir with ice and strain into a rocks glass rinsed with Green Chartreuse. Twist a lime peel over the top and discard.

Marchessa

The Independent in Somerville's addition to the Count Negroni story.

- 1 oz Plymouth Gin
- 1 oz Amaro Nonino
- 1 oz Aperol

Stir with ice and strain into a cocktail glass. Garnish with an orange twist.

Marconi Wireless No. 2

Corey Bunnewith merged the Marconi Wireless with the Green Point at Coppa in Boston.

- 2 oz Clear Creek Eau de Pome
- 1/2 oz Green Chartreuse
- 1/2 oz Punt e Mes

Stir with ice and strain into a rocks glass.

Maroquet Swizzle

Ben Sandrof served this tribute to sunrise in Martinique at his Sunday Salon speakeasy series.

- 2 oz Neisson Rhum Agricole Blanc
- 1/2 oz Grapefruit Juice
- 1/4 oz Lime Juice
- 1 dash Simple Syrup
- 1/2 oz Grenadine

Add grenadine to the bottom of a Highball glass. Gently add crushed ice and then other ingredients. Swizzle to mix while taking care not to disturb the grenadine layer on the bottom. Garnish with mint sprigs and a few drops of Pernod, and add a straw.

MA

Martin Voiron

Rick Messier crossed Martin Miller's name with the city where Chartreuse is made in this very yellow drink at No. 9 Park.

- 1 oz Martin Miller's Gin
- 1 1/4 oz Yellow Chartreuse
- 1 1/4 oz St. Germain
- 1 oz Lemon Juice
- 1 dash Fee's Grapefruit Bitters

Shake with ice and strain into a cocktail glass.

Mary Sharon

Josh Taylor with help from the Bittermens' Avery Glasser created this abstraction of the Cosmopolitan at Eastern Standard.

- 1 1/2 oz Chinaco Blanco Tequila
- 3/4 oz Martini & Rossi Bianco Vermouth
- 1/2 oz Mirto
- 1 dash Bittermens Mole Bitters

Stir with ice and strain into a cocktail glass. Garnish with a lemon twist.

Mary's Sock Drawer

Todd Maul at Clio toyed with fellow bartender Mary who in turn called the drink the Bitter Todd.

- 1 1/2 oz Bols Genever
- 1/3 oz Rhum Clément Creole Shrubb
- 1/2 oz Lime Juice
- 1/2 oz Gran Classico

Shake with ice and strain into a cocktail glass.

Max's Blood and Sand

Max Toste at Deep Ellum felt that the classic needed to be less sweet and more engaging.

- 2 oz Dewar's Blended Scotch
- 1/2 oz Cherry Heering
- 1/2 oz Martini & Rossi Sweet Vermouth
- 2 slice Orange
- 1 Luxardo Marasca Cherry
- 2 dash Orange Bitters

Muddle the cherry, orange slices, and bitters. Add rest of ingredients and ice, shake, and double strain into a cocktail glass. Garnish with a fresh orange slice and cherry.

Max's Marconi Wireless

One of the many variations on classics created by Max Toste at Deep Ellum in Allston.

❖ 1 2/3 oz Applejack
❖ 3/4 oz Sweet Vermouth
❖ 1/2 oz Maraschino Liqueur
❖ 1 Sugar Cube
❖ 1 piece Orange Peel
❖ 2 dash Orange Bitters

❖ *Muddle the sugar cube, bitters, and orange peel in a mixing glass. Add in the rest of the ingredients and ice, stir, and strain into a cocktail glass.*

Meadowlands

Misty Kalkofen paid tribute to Laird's New Jersey roots at Brick and Mortar in Cambridge.

❖ 2 oz Laird's Bonded Apple Brandy
❖ 1/2 oz Simple Syrup
❖ 1/4 oz Apricot Liqueur
❖ 1/4 oz Becherovka
❖ 1 dash Fee's Whiskey Barrel Bitters

❖ *Swizzle on crushed ice in a rocks glass. Top with more crushed ice and add straws.*

Mary Sharon,
Eastern Standard

ME

Means of Preservation

Drink's John Gertsen riffed off the Teardrop Lounge's Ephemeral.

2 oz Beefeater Gin
1/2 oz St. Germain
1/2 oz Dolin Dry Vermouth
2 dash Celery Bitters

Stir with ice and strain into a coupe glass. Garnish with a grapefruit twist.

Metamorphosis

This Czech variation of the classic Bee's Knees was one of the early drinks crafted for the Eastern Standard menu, and perhaps it is one of the most popular as well.

1 1/2 oz Becherovka
3/4 oz Lemon Juice
3/4 oz Honey Syrup

Shake with ice and strain into a cocktail glass. Garnish with a lemon twist.

Metexa (variation)

Deep Ellum's Max Toste tinkered with the Metexa that appears in the Café Royal Cocktail Book from 1937.

1 1/4 oz Cocchi Americano
3/4 oz Swedish Punsch
1/2 oz Fidencio Mezcal
1/2 oz Blanco Tequila
1 dash Lemon Juice
1 dash Orange Bitters

Stir with ice and strain into a cocktail coupe. Garnish with a lemon twist.

Mexican Love Affair

Created at Drink in Boston.

1 oz Pierre Ferrand Cognac
1 oz Domaine de Canton Ginger Liqueur
1/2 oz St. Elizabeth Allspice Dram
1/2 oz Honey Syrup
1/4 oz Lemon Juice
1 dash Tabasco Sauce

Shake with ice and strain into a cocktail glass.

Midnight Elixir

The perfect Rx for malaise served at Stoddard's.

❖
❖
❖ 2 oz Ransom Old Tom Gin
❖ 3/4 oz Lime Juice
❖ 1/2 oz Ginger Syrup
❖
❖ *Shake with ice and strain into a*
Highball glass filled with crushed
❖ *ice. Add ~1 oz soda water and float*
❖ *1/2 oz Fernet Branca. Garnish with*
❖ *a lime wheel and add a straw.*

◆

Millionaire of Havana

Dave Delaney's merged two apricot liqueur-laden classics, the Millionaire and the Havana, at Worcester's Citizen Restaurant.

❖ 1 oz Old Monk Rum
❖ 1 oz Apricot Liqueur
❖ 1 oz Swedish Punsch
❖ 1 dash Lemon Juice
❖
❖ *Stir with ice and strain into a cock-*
❖ *tail glass. Garnish with an orange*
❖ *twist.*

◆

Milord Gower

Fred Yarm's companion to the Green Chartreuse-based St. Germain from the Café Royal Cocktail Book.

❖ 1 1/2 oz Yellow Chartreuse
❖ 3/4 oz Orange Juice
❖ 3/4 oz Lime Juice
❖ 1 Egg White
❖
❖ *Shake without ice and then with ice.*
❖ *Strain into a cocktail glass and gar-*
❖ *nish with 5 drops of orange bitters.*

◆

Milwaukee Monk

Estragon's Sahil Mehta based his drink off of Coppa's Coney Island Strong Man.

❖ 2 oz Green Chartreuse
❖ 1 oz Lime Juice
❖ 2 dash Regan's Orange Bitters
❖
❖ *Shake with ice and strain into a pint*
❖ *glass. Add 12 oz Miller High Life,*
❖ *gently stir, and garnish with a lime*
❖ *wheel.*
❖

❖ Momisette Sour,
❖ Bergamot

Mission of Burma

Drink's John Gertsen thought up this inverse Pegu Club for a Grand Marnier event in 2009, and the drink helped the bar win the Barroom Brawl at Tales of the Cocktail in 2010.

❖ 2 1/4 oz Grand Marnier
❖ 1/4 oz Anchor Junipero Gin
❖ 1/4 oz Lime Juice
❖ 1/4 oz Angostura Bitters

❖ *Shake with ice and strain into a*
❖ *cocktail glass. Twist a lime peel over*
❖ *the top.*

Momisette Sour

Bergamot's modification of a classic Parisian drink, the Momisette.

❖ 2 oz Bols Genever
❖ 1/2 oz Pastis d'Autrefois
❖ 1/2 oz Lemon Juice
❖ 1/2 oz Simple Syrup
❖ 1 barspoon Orgeat
❖ 1 Egg White

❖ *Shake without ice and then with ice,*
❖ *and strain into a rocks glass. Add ice*
❖ *cubes and a straw, and garnish with*
3 drops of orange blossom water.

114

Monk's Thistle

Ryan Lotz at Lineage riffed on Ben Sandrof's Silent Order.

- ❖ 2 oz Green Chartreuse
- ❖ 1/2 oz Cynar
- ❖ 1/2 oz Water
- ❖ 2 dash Regan's Orange Bitters
- ❖
- ❖ *Stir with ice and strain into a cocktail glass.*

◆

Montmartre

Carrie Cole's French take on the Brooklyn cocktail for the Craigie on Main cocktail menu.

- ❖ 2 oz Citadelle Reserve Gin
- ❖ 1 oz Dolin Dry Vermouth
- ❖ 1/4 oz Amer Picon (or replica)
- ❖ 1/4 oz Maraschino Liqueur
- ❖
- ❖ *Stir with ice and strain into a cocktail glass. Garnish with a brandied cherry.*

◆

Monopatin

Ted Gallagher of Craigie on Main named this after the Spanish word for "skateboard" with the Peralta and Moto Guzzi as inspiration.

- ❖ 1 1/2 oz Lustau Fino Sherry
- ❖ 1 1/2 oz Rabarbaro Zucca Amaro
- ❖
- ❖ *Stir with ice and strain into a rocks glass with a mezcal rinse and a large ice cube. Garnish the ice cube with a pinch of sea salt.*

◆

Morning Glory Fizz (variation)

No. 9 Park's Ted Kilpatrick swapped a few ingredients around in Harry Johnson's vintage recipe.

- ❖ 2 oz Glenrothes Single Malt Scotch
- ❖ 3/4 oz Lemon Juice
- ❖ 3/4 oz Simple Syrup
- ❖ 1 barspoon Absinthe
- ❖ 1 Egg White
- ❖
- ❖ *Shake without ice and then with ice. Strain into a Highball glass, top with ~3 oz of St. Bernardus Tripel beer, and add a straw.*

◆

Moto Guzzi

John Gertsen mixed this simple but elegant two part drink for a motorcycle enthusiast regular at No. 9 Park.

- ❖ 1 1/2 oz Booker's Bourbon
- ❖ 1 1/2 oz Punt e Mes
- ❖
- ❖ *Stir with ice and strain into a rocks glass.*
- ❖

Mountain Dew Fizz

This Trina's Starlite Lounge drink is usually made with tequila but was served at their Cócteles Latinos event in 2011 with cachaça.

❖ 2 oz Cachaça or Tequila
❖ 1/2 oz Lime Juice
❖ 1/2 oz Agave Nectar
❖ 1 Egg White
❖
❖ *Shake without ice and then with ice. Strain into a Fizz glass containing 1 1/2 oz of Mountain Dew soda.*
◆

Mount Orohena

One of Bobby McCoy's refreshing Tikisms on the Eastern Standard menu.

❖ 2 wedge Lime (1/3 Lime)
❖ 2 sprig Mint
❖ 1 1/2 oz Amber Rum
❖ 1/2 oz Cruzan Black Strap Rum
❖ 3/4 oz Spiced Syrup
❖ 6 drop Pernod
❖ 2 dash Angostura Bitters
❖
❖ *Muddle lime and mint. Add rest of ingredients and shake with ice. Double strain into a large coupe glass filled with crushed ice and garnish with a fresh mint sprig. Add straws.*
◆

Mr. Monahan's Flip

Trina's Starlite Lounge's jab at Jimmy Lane after his nuptuals to Trina's Riley Monahan.

❖ 2 oz Laird's 7 1/2 Year Apple Brandy
❖ 1 oz Madeira
❖ 1/2 oz Canned Pumpkin Purée
❖ 1/2 oz Spiced Syrup
❖ 1 Whole Egg
❖
❖ *Shake without ice and then with ice. Strain into a wineglass and garnish with Fee's Aromatic Bitters.*
◆

Native Rose

The Franklin/Citizen's Joy Richard contributed this drink for a harvest dinner at Lineage in 2010.

❖ 1 1/2 oz Berkshire Greylock Gin
❖ 1/2 oz Combier Triple Sec
❖ 1/2 oz Mint Syrup
❖ 1/2 oz Lime Juice
❖ 5 drop Rose Water
❖
❖ *Shake with ice and strain into a cocktail glass. Top with ~1 oz dry sparkling wine and garnish with a spanked mint leaf.*

Naughty Nanny

Inspired by Scott Holliday's Bosc Word, Andrea Desrosiers crafted this recipe for a Mixology Monday event.

- ❖ 3/4 oz Beefeater Gin
- ❖ 3/4 oz Lime Juice
- ❖ 3/4 oz Rothman & Winter Pear Liqueur
- ❖ 1/2 oz Yellow Chartreuse
- ❖ 1/4 oz Ginger Syrup

Shake with ice and strain into a cocktail glass.

Navy Dock Daiquiri

Created by Will Thompson at Drink in Boston.

- ❖ 1 1/2 oz Smith & Cross Rum
- ❖ 3/4 oz Cynar
- ❖ 1/2 oz Lime Juice
- ❖ 1/4 oz Maraschino Liqueur

Shake with ice and strain into a cocktail glass.

Needle in the Hay

A Blood and Sand variation by Toro bartenders Andy McNees and Ian.

- ❖ 3/4 oz Berkshire Corn Whiskey
- ❖ 3/4 oz Cherry Heering
- ❖ 3/4 oz Martini & Rossi Rosé Vermouth
- ❖ 3/4 oz Grapefruit Juice
- ❖ 1 dash Bittermens Burlesque Bitters

Shake with ice and strain into a cocktail glass. Garnish with an orange twist.

New Jersey Flip

Eastern Standard's tribute to Laird's home state.

- ❖ 1 oz Laird's Applejack
- ❖ 1 oz Tawny Port
- ❖ 1/2 oz Galliano
- ❖ 1 dash Regan's Orange Bitters
- ❖ 1 Whole Egg

Shake without ice and then with ice. Strain into a coupe glass.

New Sensation

Bergamot's update on the classic Sensation with unknown relation to the late 80s hit.

❖ 1 1/2 oz Bols Genever
❖ 3/4 oz Maraschino Liqueur
❖ 3/4 oz Lemon Juice
❖ 1 barspoon Mint Syrup
❖ 1 handful Mint Leaves

❖ *Muddle the mint, shake with ice, and double strain into a cocktail glass. Garnish with a spanked mint leaf.*

Ninth Ward

Created by Brother Cleve in 2008 for Tales of the Cocktail with a nod to Boston's Ward 8 cocktail and in honor of New Orleans' flood-damaged 9th Ward.

❖ 1 1/2 oz Bulleit Bourbon
❖ 3/4 oz Fee's Falernum
❖ 3/4 oz Lime Juice
❖ 1/2 oz St. Germain
❖ 2 dash Peychaud's Bitters

❖ *Shake with ice and strain into a cocktail glass.*

Nonantum Cocktail

Evan Harrison's riffed on the Green Point at the Independent in Somerville.

❖ 1 1/2 oz Old Overholt Rye
❖ 3/4 oz Punt e Mes
❖ 3/4 oz Strega
❖ 1 dash Angostura Bitters
❖ 1 dash Regan's Orange Bitters

❖ *Stir with ice and strain into a cocktail glass. Garnish with a Marasca cherry.*

Norman Conquest

Scott Holliday once described this Rendezvous sparkler as, "It's just a tarted up Pimm's Cup."

❖ 2 oz Pimm's No. 1
❖ 3/4 oz Lemon Juice
❖ 1/4 oz Simple Syrup

❖ *Shake with ice and strain into a Champagne flute. Top with ~2 oz dry sparkling cider from Normandy and garnish with two slices of strawberry.*

North End, ❖
Stoddard's ❖

North End

Stoddard's crafted this tribute to a Boston neighborhood that has historically been both an Irish and Italian community.

2 oz Slieve Foy Irish Whiskey
1/2 oz Aperol
1/4 oz Amaro del Capo
2 dash Boker's Bitters

Stir with ice and strain into a rocks glass. Garnish with an orange twist.

Northern Lights

Tom Schlesinger-Guidelli invented this for the inaugural Craigie on Main cocktail menu, and it quickly became one of their most popular drinks.

1 1/2 oz Grant's Blended Scotch
3/4 oz St. Germain
1/4 oz Clear Creek Douglas Fir Eau de Vie
1/2 oz Lemon Juice
1/4 oz Orange Juice
1/4 oz Simple Syrup
2 dash Bittermens Tiki Bitters

Shake with ice and strain into a cocktail coupe. Garnish with a lemon twist.

NO-OL

Nouveau Fleur

This floral and citrus sparkler was traced back to Carrie Cole at Eastern Standard.

- ❖ 1 oz St. Germain
- ❖ 1/2 oz Chinaco Blanco Tequila
- ❖ 1/2 oz Aperol
- ❖ 1/2 oz Pink Grapefruit Juice
- ❖ 1/2 oz Lime Juice
- ❖ 1 pinch Salt

Shake with ice and strain into a large coupe glass. Top with ~2 oz dry sparkling wine.

◆

Oaxaca Moon

Bergamot's riff on Craigie on Main's Northern Lights.

- ❖ 1 1/2 oz Del Maguey Mezcal Vida
- ❖ 3/4 oz Pineau des Charentes
- ❖ 1/2 oz Zirbenz Stone Pine Liqueur
- ❖ 1/2 oz Lemon Juice
- ❖ 1/4 oz Orange Juice
- ❖ 1/4 oz Simple Syrup
- ❖ 1 dash Cocktail Kingdom Falernum Bitters

Shake with ice and strain into a rocks glass containing ice cubes. Garnish with a lemon twist.

◆

O.G.

The Original Gangster created at Trina's Starlite Lounge in Somerville.

- ❖ 1 1/2 oz Beija Cachaça
- ❖ 1/2 oz Monin Orgeat
- ❖ 3/4 oz Orange Juice
- ❖ 1/2 oz Lime Juice
- ❖ 3 dash Cocktail Kingdom Falernum Bitters

Shake with ice and pour into a rocks glass. Garnish with an orange wheel and a cherry.

◆

Old Trousers

One of the beer cocktails on the menu at The Gallows in Boston.

- ❖ 1 oz Old Monk Rum
- ❖ 1/2 oz Honey Syrup
- ❖ 1 dash Fee's Aromatic Bitters

Build in a small (10 oz) snifter glass. Top with ~7 oz Guinness Stout and garnish with a healthy pinch of grated cinnamon.

One-Armed French Hooker

Emma Hollander of Trina's Starlite Lounge offered this colorfully named drink at a Bols Genever industry event at the Franklin Southie.

- ❖ 1 1/2 oz Bols Genever
- ❖ 1 oz St. Germain
- ❖ 1 oz Grapefruit Juice
- ❖ 2 dash Peychaud's Bitters

❖ *Shake with ice and strain into a cocktail glass. Top with ~1 oz prosecco.*

One for Jimmy

No. 9 Park's Tyler Wang presented this smokey Mamie Taylor-inspired drink for a J.D. Salinger-themed charity event at the Hawthorne in 2012.

- ❖ 1 3/4 oz Amontillado Sherry
- ❖ 1/4 oz Laphroaig Scotch
- ❖ 1/4 oz Maraschino Liqueur
- ❖ 1/2 oz Lime Juice

❖ *Shake with ice and strain into a Highball glass filled with fresh ice cubes. Top with 2-3 oz ginger beer, garnish with a lime twist, and add a straw.*

Orange Scaffa

A 19th century style of drink revisited by Fred Yarm for a Mixoloseum room-temperature cocktail event.

- ❖ 1 oz Beefeater Gin
- ❖ 3/4 oz Grand Marnier
- ❖ 1/4 oz Angostura Bitters
- ❖ 1/4 oz Peychaud's Bitters
- ❖ 1/4 oz Orange Bitters

❖ *Stir without ice and pour into a cocktail coupe or rocks glass. Garnish with an orange twist. Note: this is a room-temperature cocktail.*

Oregon Trail

J.B. Bernstein at Backbar paid tribute to the old computer game and Ransom Distillery's locale.

- ❖ 1 3/4 oz Ransom Old Tom Gin
- ❖ 1/2 oz Yellow Charteuse
- ❖ 1/2 oz Zirbenz Stone Pine Liqueur
- ❖ 1/4 oz Soberano Spanish Brandy
- ❖ 4 drop Scrappy's Lavender Bitters

❖ *Stir with ice and strain into a cocktail glass. Twist a lemon peel over the top.*

Orinoco

A coffee and bitters-laden Flip created by Ted Kilpatrick at No. 9 Park and named after a fertile river basin full of coffee plantations.

❖ 2 oz Rittenhouse 100 Rye
❖ 1/2 oz Angostura Bitters
❖ 1/2 oz Espresso (cooled)
❖ 3/4 oz Simple Syrup
❖ 1 Whole Egg

Shake without ice and then with ice. Strain into a rocks glass and garnish with a dusting of finely ground coffee.

Pacific Daylight

Adapted from a drink created by Carrie Cole at Eastern Standard.

❖ 3/4 oz DonQ White Rum
❖ 3/4 oz Chinaco Blanco Tequila
❖ 3/4 oz Lime Juice
❖ 1/2 oz Triple Sec
❖ 1 heaping barspoon Strawberry Preserves

Shake with ice and double strain into a cocktail glass.

The B Side's Pamlico, Eastern Standard

122

Palmyra

Created by Tom Mastricola, this is one of the earliest, most popular, and longest running drinks on the No. 9 Park menu.

- ❖ 1 1/2 oz Rain Vodka
- ❖ 3/4 oz Lime Juice
- ❖ 3/4 oz Mint Syrup

❖ *Shake with ice and strain into a cocktail glass. Garnish with a lime wedge laid over a paired segment of mint leaves such that it looks like a winged bird on the edge of the glass.*

Pamlico

Dave Cagle based this drink off of a Cuba Libre while at the old B Side Lounge in Cambridge, and it later appeared on the Eastern Standard menu.

- ❖ 1 1/2 oz DonQ White Rum
- ❖ 3/4 oz Beefeater Gin
- ❖ 3/4 oz Lime Juice
- ❖ 1 dash Angostura Bitters

❖ *Shake with ice and pour into a Highball glass. Top with ~2 oz ginger beer, garnish with a lime wedge, and add a straw.*

Panacea

John Gertsen of Drink riffed on Sam Ross' Penicillin to create this drink named after the Greek goddess of healing.

- ❖ 2 oz Banks Rum
- ❖ 1/2 oz Ginger Honey Syrup
- ❖ 1/2 oz Lime Juice

❖ *Shake with ice and strain into a rocks glass rinsed with Batavia Arrack.*

Pare de Sufrir

Misty Kalkofen then of Drink published this recipe in Beta Cocktails.

- ❖ 1 1/2 oz Lustau Pedro Ximénez Sherry
- ❖ 5/8 oz Chichicapa Mezcal
- ❖ 1/2 oz Galliano Ristretto Coffee Liqueur
- ❖ 1/4 oz Amaro Lucano
- ❖ 1 dash Angostura Bitters
- ❖ 1 dash Bitter Truth Aromatic Bitters

❖ *Stir without ice and pour into an espresso cup. Garnish with a small amount of grated canela. Note: this is a room-temperature cocktail.*

Parisian Orchid

Created by Misty Kalkofen at Green Street in Cambridge.

❖ 1 oz Vodka
❖ 1 oz St. Germain
❖ 1/2 oz Lemon Juice
❖ 1/2 oz Pineapple Juice

❖ *Shake with ice and strain into a*
❖ *cocktail glass.*

Park Street Cup

Ted Kilpatrick's tribute to the country's first subway stop located a mere block from No. 9 Park.

❖ 1 oz Pimm's No. 1
❖ 3/4 oz Peychaud's Bitters
❖ 1/2 oz Lemon Juice
❖ 3/4 oz Simple Syrup
❖ 1/4 oz Angostura Bitters
❖ 1/4 oz Fee's Orange Bitters
❖ 1 Egg White

❖ *Shake without ice and then with ice.*
❖ *Strain into a Highball glass, top*
❖ *with 3 oz of Weihenstephaner*
❖ *Hefeweizen beer, and add a straw.*

Patrician

Part of the Flight of Heraldry along with the Negroni and Contessa created by Ben Gertsen, Ryan McGrale, and Courtney Bissonnette at No. 9 Park.

❖ 1 oz Beefeater Gin
❖ 1 oz Punt e Mes
❖ 1 oz Cointreau

❖ *Stir with ice and strain into a cock-*
❖ *tail glass. Garnish with an orange*
❖ *twist.*

Peniques

A copper-colored drink by Fred Yarm that was published in The Mutineer Magazine.

❖ 1 1/2 oz Reposado Tequila
❖ 3/4 oz Ramazzotti
❖ 3/4 oz Orange Juice
❖ 1 barspoon Cinnamon Syrup
❖ 1 dash Orange Bitters

❖ *Shake with ice and strain into a*
❖ *cocktail glass. Garnish with an*
❖ *orange twist.*

Penny Reel

Stoddard's in Boston took a few classic cocktail ingredients and curiously crafted a Tiki-styled drink out of them.

❖ 1 oz Drambuie
❖ 1 oz Brandy
❖ 1 oz El Dorado 12 Year Rum
❖ 1/2 oz Lime Juice
❖ 1/4 oz Cinnamon Syrup
❖ 1/4 oz Falernum
❖ 3 dash Angostura Bitters
❖ 6-8 Raspberries (1/2 oz Purée)
❖
❖ *Muddle raspberries. Add rest of the ingredients and ice, shake, and double strain into a Tiki mug filled with crushed ice. Garnish with a lime twist and cherry, and add a straw.*

Peralta

Evan Harrison then of Deep Ellum presented this skateboarder tribute at the Bartenders on the Rise event held at Green Street in 2010.

❖ 3/4 oz Old Overholt Rye
❖ 3/4 oz Cynar
❖ 3/4 oz Yellow Chartreuse
❖ 1/2 oz Grapefruit Juice
❖ 1/4 oz Lemon Juice
❖ 1 dash Aromatic Bitters
❖
❖ *Shake with ice and strain into a coupe glass. Garnish with a grapefruit twist.*

Perfect Hand

Craigie on Main's Ted Gallagher's variation on the Milk & Honey and Little Branch's Left Hand.

❖ 1 1/2 oz Bols Genever
❖ 1/2 oz Aperol
❖ 1/4 oz Carpano Sweet Vermouth
❖ 1/4 oz Dolin Dry Vermouth
❖ 1 dash Bittermens Mole Bitters
❖
❖ *Stir with ice and strain into a cocktail glass. Garnish with an orange twist.*

Perfect Pal

This riff on the Old Pal was created by Evan Harrison and friends at the Independent in Somerville.

❖ 1 oz Old Overholt Rye
❖ 1/2 oz Cinzano Sweet Vermouth
❖ 1/2 oz Noilly Prat Dry Vermouth
❖ 1 oz Aperol
❖ 2 dash Regan's Orange Bitters
❖
❖ *Stir with ice and strain into a glass.*

Periodista

A classic Cuban drink that got adopted and adapted by Boston bartenders. Cocktail detective Devin Hahn traced the roots back to Chez Henri in Cambridge.

1 1/2 oz Gosling's or Myer's Dark Rum
1/2 oz Triple Sec
1/2 oz Apricot Brandy
1/2 oz Lime Juice

Shake with ice and strain into a cocktail glass.

Peter's Gin Flip

A nightcap Flip by Ryan Lotz at Lineage with respects paid to Peter Heering.

2 oz CapRock Gin
1 oz Cherry Heering
1 Whole Egg

Shake without ice and then with ice. Strain into a rocks glass and garnish with either Bittermens Mole Bitters or freshly grated nutmeg.

Petition

Influenced by No. 9's Petion variation, the Soekarno, Fred Yarm created this nod to Leblon's efforts to legalize cachaça as its own spirit class.

3/4 oz Cachaça
3/4 oz Bénédictine
3/4 oz Lime Juice
3/4 oz Dry Vermouth
1/4 oz Simple Syrup
1 dash Angostura Bitters

Shake with ice and strain into a cocktail glass. Garnish with a lime twist.

Phipp's Fizz

Dylan Black's classic-styled Highball on the Green Street menu.

2 oz Old Overholt Rye
1/2 oz Lemon Juice
1 dash Angostura Bitters

Shake with ice and strain into a Highball glass filled with ice. Top with 2-3 oz AJ Stephans Ginger Beer and garnish with a lemon wedge.

Pineapple Tree

An easy drinking Highball created by Ben Sandrof at his Sunday Salon speakeasy series.

❖ 1 1/2 oz Neisson Rhum Agricole
❖   Blanc
❖ 3/4 oz Pineapple Syrup
❖ 3/4 oz Lime Juice
❖
❖ *Shake with ice and strain into a*
❖ *Collins glass filled with ice cubes.*
❖ *Top with soda water and add a*
❖ *straw. Garnish with a few dashes of*
❖ *Angostura Bitters, a wide lime twist,*
◆ *and a pineapple fruit leaf.*

Pink Poodle

The classic Pink Lady's pooch found its way over to Toro in Boston.

❖ 2 oz Beija Cachaça
❖ 1 oz Grenadine
❖ 1/2 oz Lemon Juice
❖ 1/2 oz Lime Juice
❖ 1 Egg White
❖
❖ *Shake without ice and then with ice.*
❖ *Strain into a rocks glass partially*
❖ *filled with fresh ice, garnish with a*
❖ *cherry, and add a straw.*

Pineapple Tree,
Sunday Salon

127

Plainfield Swing

A tribute to jazz great Bill Evans by John Mayer while at Craigie on Main.

1 1/2 oz Laird's Bonded Apple Brandy
1/2 oz Bénédictine
1/2 oz Triple Sec
1/2 oz Lemon Juice
1 dash St. Elizabeth Allspice Dram

Shake with ice and strain into a cocktail glass. Garnish with freshly grated cinnamon.

Pokey Crocus

Fred Yarm won the Spring-themed Drinking in America contest in 2012 with this recipe.

2 oz Dry Gin
1/2 oz Green Tea Syrup
1/2 oz Dry Vermouth
1 barspoon Crème de Violette

Stir with ice and strain into a cocktail glass.

Ponce de Leon

Bobby McCoy honored the search for the fountain of youth at Eastern Standard.

2 oz Berkshire Ragged Mountain Rum
1 oz Lustau East India Solera Sherry
1/2 oz Licor 43
1 dash Orange Bitters

Stir with ice and strain into a rocks glass. Garnish with a flamed orange twist.

Ponte Vecchio

A digestif by Sam Treadway served at Backbar in Somerville.

1 1/4 oz Cynar
1 1/4 oz Fernet Branca
1/2 oz Lemon Juice

Stir with ice and strain into a coupe glass. Garnish with a lemon twist.

Posta Aerea

A Campari riff on the classic Air Mail from Craigie on Main.

- 1 oz Campari
- 1/2 oz Lemon Juice
- 1/2 oz Honey Syrup

Shake with ice and strain into a Champagne flute. Top with 2-3 oz sparkling wine and garnish with a lemon twist.

Potaro Punch

Created by Misty Kalkofen.

- 1 3/4 oz Demerara Rum
- 1/2 oz Becherovka
- 1/2 oz Lapsang Souchong Tea Syrup
- 1/4 oz Lemon Juice

Shake with ice and strain into a cocktail glass.

Pride of the Neighborhood

At Craigie on Main, John Mayer was inspired by Steely Dan's song "Josie," and he offered the curious subtitle "Donald Fagen is a Vampire."

- 1 1/2 oz Bols Genever
- 1 oz Averna
- 1/2 oz Cherry Heering
- 1/4+ oz Blackberry Syrup
- 2 dash Mole Bitters
- 1 Whole Egg

Shake without ice and then with ice. Strain into a coupe glass and garnish with 8 drops of Tiki Bitters. Instead of the blackberry syrup, muddle a blackberry in 1/4 oz simple syrup and add a fine straining step.

Prince of Orange

Estragon's Sahil Mehta developed this recipe for an article on Genever drinks.

- 1 1/2 oz Bols Genever
- 1 oz Drambuie
- 1/2 oz Lemon Juice
- 1/4 oz Orange Juice
- 1 tsp Orange Marmalade
- 2 dash Angostura Bitters

Shake with ice and double strain into a coupe glass. Garnish with an orange twist.

129

❖ Purkhart's Peck,
❖ Franklin Café

Principe Eduardo

A tequila cocktail by Misty Kalkofen when she was at Drink that was inspired by the classic Prince Edward.

❖ 2 oz El Tesoro Reposado Tequila
❖ 3/4 oz Lillet Blanc
❖ 1/4 oz Drambuie
❖ 1 dash Angostura Bitters
❖ 1 dash Angostura Orange Bitters

Stir with ice and strain into a cocktail glass. Twist a lemon peel over the top.

Prison Nickname

Careful of what you ask for at Local 149, sweetcheeks; crafted by John Mayer.

❖ 1 1/2 oz Pimm's No. 1
❖ 1/2 oz Lemon Juice
❖ 1/4 oz Crème de Cassis

Shake with ice and strain into a rocks glass. Top with ~5 oz Ommegang Belgian-style Pale Ale and garnish with a few spritzes (or several drops) of Fernet Branca Menta.

Prospect Park

One of Eastern Standard's early Manhattan variations.

❖
❖ 1 1/2 oz Rittenhouse 100 Rye
❖ 1 1/2 oz Aperol
❖ 1/2 oz Maraschino Liqueur
❖ 1/2 oz Punt e Mes.
❖

❖ *Stir with ice and strain into a cock-*
❖ *tail glass. Garnish with a Marasca*
❖ *cherry.*

◆

Pulitzer

Eastern Standard's tribute to award winning writers everywhere.

❖ 1 oz Bulleit Rye
❖ 1 oz Martini & Rossi Sweet
❖   Vermouth
❖ 1 oz Aperol
❖

❖ *Stir with ice and strain into a cock-*
❖ *tail glass. Garnish with an orange*
❖ *twist.*

◆

Purkhart's Peck

Served at the Franklin Southie for a Buffalo Trace and Eagle Rare industry night in 2010.

❖ 1 1/2 oz Eagle Rare Bourbon
❖ 1/2 oz Rothman & Winter Apricot
❖   Liqueur
❖ 1/2 oz Dolin Dry Vermouth
❖ 2 dash Jerry Thomas Decanter
❖   Bitters
❖

❖ *Stir with ice and strain into a cock-*
❖ *tail glass. Garnish with an orange*
❖ *twist.*

◆

Queen's Smile

Bergamot in Somerville's riff on the Prince's Smile.

❖ 1 1/2 oz Beefeater Gin
❖ 1/2 oz Drambuie
❖ 1/2 oz Lemon Juice
❖ 1/2 oz Rothman & Winter Apricot
❖   Liqueur
❖

❖ *Shake with ice and strain into a*
❖ *cocktail glass. Garnish with a lemon*
❖ *twist.*
❖

Rabbit Stick

Scott Holliday's reworking of the Savoy Cocktail Book's Boomerang at Rendezvous.

- ❖ 2 oz Rittenhouse 100 Rye
- ❖ 1 oz Swedish Punsch
- ❖ 1/2 oz Noilly Prat Dry Vermouth
- ❖ 2 dash Angostura Bitters
- ❖ 2 dash Angostura Orange Bitters
- ❖
- ❖ *Stir with ice and strain into a rocks glass. Twist a lemon peel over the top.*

Rabo‑de‑Galo

Hugh Fiore offered his take on a classic Brazilian cocktail at Eastern Standard in Boston.

- ❖ 2 oz Beija Cachaça
- ❖ 1 oz Punt e Mes
- ❖ 1 dash Orange Bitters
- ❖
- ❖ *Stir with ice and strain into a cocktail glass rinsed with St. Elizabeth Allspice Dram. Twist an orange peel over the top.*

Rapa Nui

Inspired by the history of Easter Island, Kit Paschal crafted this drink for Eastern Standard's Tikisms section of the menu.

- ❖ 1 1/2 oz Old Monk Rum
- ❖ 1/2 oz Smith & Cross Rum
- ❖ 2 oz Blood Orange Juice
- ❖ 1/2 oz Lime Juice
- ❖ 1/2 oz Cinnamon Syrup
- ❖ 1/4 oz Bauchant Orange Liqueur
- ❖
- ❖ *Shake with ice and strain into a water goblet filled with crushed ice. Float 1/2 oz of Lustau East India Solera Sherry. Garnish with an orange slice and cherry, and add straws.*

Rapscallion

Created by Tyler Wang at Drink for a 19th century pub crawl hosted by Sarah Lohman of the Four Pounds Flour blog.

- ❖ 1 oz Dry Oloroso Sherry
- ❖ 1 oz Averna
- ❖ 3/4 oz Galliano Ristretto Coffee Liqueur
- ❖ 1/4 oz Old Port Rum
- ❖ 3 dash Mole Bitters
- ❖
- ❖ *Stir without ice and pour into a punch cup. Top with a meringue made with an egg white, 1/4 oz Mole Bitters, and a 1/4 tsp sugar. Garnish with freshly grated coffee bean and lemon oil from a twist.*

Red Rot Cocktail

DrinkBoston's Lauren Clark and then Green Street bartender Misty Kalkofen contributed this recipe to the Boston Athenaeum's Roaring Twenties event in 2007.

1 1/2 oz Dry Gin
1/2 oz St. Germain
1/2 oz Cherry Heering
1/2 oz Lemon Juice
2 dash Peychaud's Bitters

Shake with ice and strain into a cocktail glass.

Red Sea

Brendan Pratt came up with the recipe at Lineage and the staff dubbed it as a reference to his nickname, Moses.

1 1/2 oz Beefeater Gin
3/4 oz Campari
1/2 oz Plymouth Sloe Gin
1 barspoon Combier Triple Sec
2 dash Orange Bitters

Stir with ice and strain into a rocks glass. Twist a grapefruit peel over the top.

Remedy

Joy Richard offered this cure-all for a St. Germain industry night at the Franklin Southie.

1 oz Sazerac 6 Year Rye
3/4 oz St. Germain
1/2 oz Yellow Chartreuse
1/4 oz Fernet Branca

Stir with ice and strain into a cocktail glass. Garnish with a lemon twist.

Revision Cocktail

At the Citizen Public House in Boston, bar manager Joy Richard was trying to come up with a sherry aperitif, but it took a few tries.

1 1/2 oz Lustau Dry Amontillado Sherry
1 oz Dolin Dry Vermouth
1/2 oz Combier Triple Sec
2 dash Bittermens Grapefruit Bitters

Stir with ice and strain into a cocktail glass. Garnish with a lemon twist.

Rhum Cocktail Marilene

Scott Holliday created this drink at Chez Henri and brought it with him for Rendezvous' menu.

- 2 oz Barbancourt 8 Year Rum
- 1/2 Lime (4 pieces)
- 2 tsp Sugar
- 2 dash Angostura Bitters

Muddle the lime pieces and sugar in a rocks glass, add rum and ice, and shake. Add Angostura bitters on top and lightly stir in.

Riccardo

A mezcal take on the classic Blood and Sand named after one of the regulars at Coppa in Boston.

- 3/4 oz Del Maguey Crema de Mezcal
- 3/4 oz Cherry Heering
- 3/4 oz Orange Juice
- 3/4 oz Cinzano Sweet Vermouth
- 1 dash Hot Pepper Sauce

Shake with ice and strain into a rocks glass filled with fresh ice. Garnish with a cherry. Substitute 3/4 oz regular mezcal plus 1/2 tsp agave nectar for the Crema.

Rickshaw

Created at Highland Kitchen in Somerville.

- 1 oz Laird's Applejack
- 1 oz Domaine de Canton Ginger Liqueur
- 1/2 oz Orange Juice
- 1/2 oz Lemon Juice

Shake with ice and strain into a sugar-rimmed cocktail glass. Garnish with a large pickled ginger slice.

Rome is Burning

A sparkling aperitif by Scott Holliday at Rendezvous in Cambridge.

- 1 1/2 oz Cognac
- 3/4 oz Punt e Mes
- 1/4 oz Grenadine
- 3 dash Peychaud's Bitters

Stir with ice and strain into a cocktail glass. Top with ~1 1/2 oz Lambrusco.

Roots of Rum,
Backbar

Root of All Evil

Eastern Standard conjured some Tiki flare in this root beer-flavored Flip.

1 oz Root Liqueur
1 oz Spiced Rum
1 oz Coconut Cream
2 dash Angostura Orange Bitters
1 Whole Egg

Shake without ice and then with ice. Strain into a coupe glass.

Roots of Rum

A Tiki libation from Backbar in Somerville.

2 oz El Dorado 12 Year Rum
1/2 oz Root Liqueur
1/2 oz Lime Juice
1/2 oz Fee's Orgeat
1/2 oz Ginger Syrup

Shake with ice and strain into a rocks glass filled with crushed ice. Garnish with a floated lime wheel, dash Angostura Bitters to the top of the lime wheel, and add straws.

135

Roxbury Russet

Created by Carl Donheiser at The Gallows in Boston and named after one of the oldest apple cultivars that was discovered a mile or so away from the bar.

- ❖ 1 oz Cognac
- ❖ 1/2 oz Laird's Applejack
- ❖ 1/2 oz Lemon Juice
- ❖ 1/2 oz Honey Syrup
- ❖ 4 dash Fee's Aromatic Bitters
- ❖ 3-4 slice Apple (~1/6 medium apple)

Muddle 4 cloves. Add apple slices and muddle again. Add rest of ingredients and ice, shake, and double strain into a cocktail glass. Garnish with an additional apple slice.

Rude Boy

Rendezvous' Scott Holliday came up with a drink that reminded him of the cologne that a 1960's Jamaican Rude Boy might wear.

- ❖ 2 oz Wray & Nephew Overproof White Rum
- ❖ 3/4 oz Lime Juice
- ❖ 1/2 oz Simple Syrup
- ❖ 1/4 oz S. Maria al Monte Amaro

Shake ingredients with ice and strain into a cocktail glass. Garnish with 3 drops of orange blossom water and a lime wedge.

Rumbustion Flip

A Flip crafted by Misty Kalkofen at Drink.

- ❖ 1 1/2 oz St. Ambroise Oatmeal Stout
- ❖ 1 oz Old Monk Rum
- ❖ 1/2 oz St. Elizabeth Allspice Dram
- ❖ 1/2 oz Simple Syrup
- ❖ 1 Whole Egg

Shake without ice and then with ice. Strain into a rocks glass and garnish with several drops of Fee's Whiskey Barrel Bitters.

Rum Scaffa

Scott Holliday became inspired by old school Scaffa drinks and crafted this one at Rendezvous in Cambridge.

- ❖ 1 1/2 oz Plantation Barbados Rum
- ❖ 1 1/2 oz Cynar
- ❖ 1 dash Angostura Orange Bitters

Stir without ice and pour into a cocktail glass. Note: this is a room-temperature drink.

Rye and Dry

Eastern Standard riffed on the classic Rye and Dry for the Pimm's section of their menu back in 2008.

❖ 1 oz Sazerac 6 Year Rye
❖ 1 oz Pimm's No. 1
❖ 1 oz Dry Vermouth
❖ 1 dash Bittermens Mole Bitters

❖ *Stir with ice and strain into a rocks glass.*

Sacrilege

Created by John McElroy of Russell House Tavern.

❖ 1 1/2 oz John L. Sullivan Irish
❖   Whiskey
❖ 1 oz Cardamaro
❖ 1/2 oz Sweet Vermouth
❖ 1/2 oz Lemon Juice
❖ 1/2 oz Honey Syrup

❖ *Shake with ice and strain into a rocks glass.*

Saint Bruno Swizzle

Hawthorne's Scott Marshall paid tribute to the founder of the Carthusian Order.

❖ 1 oz Batavia Arrack
❖ 1/2 oz Green Chartreuse
❖ 1/2 oz Yellow Chartreuse
❖ 1/2 oz Lemon Juice
❖ 1/2 oz Lime Juice

❖ *Build over crushed ice in a Collins glass and swizzle to mix and chill. Float 1/2 oz Plantation Barbados Rum, garnish with 2 dashes Bittermens Mole Bitters, and add a straw.*

Saloon Man's Sour

Crafted at Craigie on Main by Tom Schlesinger-Guidelli with the subtitle "New England warmth, tropical aroma."

❖ 1 1/2 oz Sailor Jerry's Spiced Rum
❖ 1/2 oz Plymouth Sloe Gin
❖ 1/2 oz Lime Juice
❖ 1/4 oz Maple Syrup
❖ 2 dash Peychaud's Bitters

❖ *Shake with ice and strain into a rocks glass.*

Sands of Time

Created by Todd Maul of Clio in Boston.

❖ 1 1/2 oz Bols Genever
❖ 1/2 oz Punt e Mes
❖ 1/2 oz Cherry Heering
❖ 1/2 oz Pimm's No. 1
❖ 1/2 oz Lemon Juice
❖ 1/4 oz Simple Syrup
❖ 1 dash Jerry Thomas Decanter
   Bitters
❖

❖ Stir with ice and strain into a coupe glass. Garnish with a marigold petal if in season.

San Francisco Nog

Adapted from a drink created by Deep Ellum for their 2010 Winter menu that honors the United States' Fernet capital.

◆ 1 1/2 oz Fernet Branca
❖ 3/4 oz Heavy Cream
❖ 3/4 oz Simple Syrup
❖ 1 Egg Yolk
❖ 1 Sugar Cube

❖ Muddle sugar cube and add the rest of the ingredients. Shake with ice and strain into a rocks glass. Garnish with freshly grated nutmeg.

Sands of Time, Clio

Sangre du Nord

For the Museum of Fine Arts' 2006 "Americans in Paris" exhibit, No. 9 Park riffed on the classic Monkey Gland. Adapted from Food & Wine: Cocktails 2007.

❖ 2 oz Gin
❖ 1 oz Orange Juice
❖ 1/2 oz Cointreau
❖ 1/4 oz Pernod Pastis

❖ Shake with ice and strain into a cocktail glass.

Sao Paulo Summer

Deep Ellum's Brazilian-themed drink using a honey-ginger syrup they had in house for a Penicillin variation.

◆ 2 oz Germana Aged Cachaça
3/4 oz Ginger Honey Syrup
1/2 oz Lime Juice
❖ 2 sprig Mint (leaves only)
1 wedge Lime

Shake with ice and pour into a rocks glass without straining. Add straws.

Saucy Sureau

A riff on the classic Saucy Sue adapted from LUPEC Boston's Little Black Book of Cocktails.

◆ 1 oz Lecompte Originel Calvados
3/4 oz St. Germain
3/4 oz Lemon Juice
❖ 1/4 oz Rothman & Winter Apricot Liqueur

Shake with ice and strain into a cocktail glass.

Saveur d'Elegance

Hugh Fiore created this bitter sweet sparkler at Eastern Standard.

◆ 3/4 oz Aperol
❖ 3/4 oz Mirto
3/4 oz Lillet Blanc

Stir with ice and strain into a Champagne flute. Top with ~2 oz sparkling wine and garnish with an orange twist.

Scarlet Swizzle

A Swizzle crafted around a flavorful Trinidad Rum at the Citizen Public House in Boston.

❖ 2 oz Scarlet Ibis Rum
❖ 1/2 oz Yellow Chartreuse
❖ 1 1/2 oz Grapefruit Juice
❖ 1/2 oz Cinnamon Syrup
❖ 4 dash Bittermens Tiki Bitters
❖
❖ *Build in a Collins glass. Add crushed ice and swizzle until the glass begins to frost over. Garnish with a grapefruit twist and a barspoon of St. Elizabeth Allspice Dram. Add a straw.*

Scotland the Brave

No. 9 Park's Ted Kilpatrick dubbed his creation after the unofficial national anthem of Scotland.

❖ 2 oz Laphroaig 10 Year Scotch
❖ 3/4 oz Fernet Branca
❖ 3/4 oz Punt e Mes
❖ 1/2 oz Mathilde Orange Liqueur
❖
❖ *Stir with ice and strain into a rocks glass. Flame an orange peel over the top.*

Scottish Play

Named after Shakespeare's Macbeth, I surmise that Russell House Tavern's Aaron Butler was influenced by his fascination then with Punchdrunk's Sleep No More production.

❖ 1 3/4 oz Laphroaig 10 Year Scotch
❖ 1 1/4 oz Cynar
❖ 1 oz Aperol
❖ 1/8 oz Drambuie
❖
❖ *Stir with ice and strain into a rocks glass. Twist an orange peel over the top.*

Seek_No_ Further

Created by Misty Kalkofen for Drink's Smokey Sunday theme and named after an old Massachusetts heirloom apple variety.

❖ 2 oz Laird's 7 1/2 Year Apple Brandy
❖ 1/2 oz Bénédictine
❖ 1/2 oz Simple Syrup
❖ 3 dash Angostura Bitters
❖
❖ *Stir the ingredient with ice. Meanwhile, pour 1/2 oz Laphroaig Cask Strength Scotch into a coupe and ignite. Twist an orange peel over the fire and drop in to carmelize.*
❖ *Strain the drink into the glass to extinguish the fire.*

Sentimental Gentleman

A rich Scotch drink by Misty Kalkofen at Brick and Mortar.

2 oz Douglas XO Blended Scotch
1/2 oz Bénédictine
1/2 oz Nux Alpina Walnut Liqueur

Stir with ice and strain into a rocks glass.

Shaddock

Josh Childs' libation served at both Trina's Starlite Lounge and Silvertone was named after the grapefruit-like citrus fruit brought to the Caribbean by Captain Shaddock.

3/4 oz Bols Genever
3/4 oz St. Germain
3/4 oz Aperol
3/4 oz Lemon Juice

Shake with ice and strain into a cocktail glass. Garnish with a lemon twist.

Shadow Play

An adaptation of a recipe created by California Gold at Drink in Boston.

1 oz Batavia Arrack
1 oz Montecristo 12 Year Rum
1/2 oz Lime Juice
1/2 oz Ferrara Orgeat
1 Egg White

Shake without ice and then with ice. Strain into a coupe glass and garnish with a few drops each of Peychaud's Bitters and Herbsaint.

Shiver

One of Rob Kraemer's house originals at Cambridge's Chez Henri.

1 1/2 oz Campari
1 1/2 oz Grapefruit Juice
1/2 oz Clear Creek Douglas Fir Eau de Vie

Shake with ice and strain into a cocktail glass. Garnish with an orange slice.

SI

Sicilian Sour

Sam Treadway at Drink based this Sour off of something he was served in Paris.

* 1 1/2 oz Rittenhouse 100 Rye
* 1/2 oz Averna
* 1/2 oz Galliano Ristretto Coffee Liqueur
* 1/2 oz Lemon Juice
* 2 dash Angostura Bitters
* 1 Egg White

Shake without ice and then with ice. Strain into a rocks glass and garnish with 3 coffee beans.

Sierra Madre

Created at No. 9 Park in Boston.

* 2 oz Milagro Silver Tequila
* 3/4 oz St. Elizabeth Allspice Dram
* 3/4 oz Crème de Cacao
* 1/2 oz Orange Juice
* 1/2 oz Lemon Juice
* 2 dash Regan's Orange Bitters

Shake with ice and strain into a cocktail glass.

Silent Order

Ben Sandrof's tribute to the ever quiet Carthusian Monks who make Chartreuse.

* 2 oz Green Chartreuse
* 1/2 oz Lime Juice
* 1/2 oz Water
* 7-10 Sweet Basil Leaves

Shake with ice and double strain into a cocktail glass.

Simon

Todd Maul named this after a regular at Clio and barfly around town.

* 2 oz Rittenhouse 100 Rye
* 1/2 oz Averna
* 1/2 oz Lemon Juice
* 1/4 oz Cherry Heering
* 1 dash Fee's Chocolate Bitters

Shake with ice and strain into a coupe glass.

Sinu Metu

Joy Richardson developed this drink for a Jameson St. Patty's Day industry event at the Franklin Southie.

❖ 1 1/2 oz Jameson Irish Whiskey
❖ 1 oz Lillet Blanc
❖ 1/2 oz Cherry Heering
❖ 3 dash Jerry Thomas Decanter Bitters

Stir with ice and strain into a cocktail glass. Garnish with a brandied cherry.

Sister Mary

Perhaps a riff on her Bohemian, Misty Kalkofen came up with this popular number at Brick and Mortar.

❖ 1 oz Chinaco Blanco Tequila
❖ 1 oz St. Germain
❖ 3/4 oz Grapefruit Juice
❖ 1/4 oz Aperol

Shake with ice and strain into a cocktail coupe.

Sister Mary, Brick & Mortar

Skipper's Flip

Derric Crothers converted the hot Skipper's Punch on the Green Street menu into a tasty Flip.

❖ 1 1/2 oz Myer's Dark Rum
❖ 1/2 oz Bénédictine
❖ 1/2 oz Lime Juice
❖ 1/2 oz Spiced Brown Sugar Syrup
❖ 1 dash Bittermens Tiki Bitters
❖ 1 Whole Egg

❖ *Shake without ice and then with ice.*
❖ *Strain into a wine glass and garnish*
❖ *with freshly grated nutmeg. Regular*
❖ *brown sugar syrup will substitute in a*
❖ *pinch.*

Skipper's Punch

Green Street owner Dylan Black adapted the Skipper's Particular in Esquire's Handbook for Hosts into this delightful Winter treat.

◆ 1 1/2 oz Myer's Dark Rum
❖ 1/2 oz Bénédictine
❖ 1/4 oz Spiced Brown Sugar Syrup
❖ 1/4 oz Lime Juice

❖ *Add to an Irish Coffee Mug and stir*
❖ *to mix. Fill with ~3 oz of boiling*
❖ *water. Regular brown sugar syrup*
❖ *will substitute in a pinch.*

Sloe 75

Jennifer Salucci's wild riff on a French 75 that she developed at Deep Ellum in Allston.

◆ 1 oz Gin
❖ 3/4 oz Bitter Truth Sloe Gin
❖ 1/2 oz Aperol
❖ 1/2 oz Lime Juice
❖ 1/4 oz Simple Syrup
❖ 2 dash Orange Bitters

❖ *Shake with ice and strain into a wine*
❖ *glass. Top with 2 oz of prosecco.*
Garnish with a wide lime twist.
◆

Smoking Jacket

A nightcap from Paul Manzelli of Somerville's Bergamot.

❖ 1 1/2 oz Grant's Blended Scotch
❖ 3/4 oz Cynar
❖ 3/4 oz Punt e Mes
❖ 2 dash Orange Bitters

❖ *Stir with ice and strain into a rocks*
❖ *glass containing a large ice cube.*
Flame an orange twist over the top.
❖

Snap Point

A Winter aperitif loaded with Alpine spice by Bobby McCoy at Island Creek Oyster Bar.

- 1 1/2 oz Ransom Old Tom Gin
- 1 1/2 oz Bonal Gentiane-Quinquina
- 1 barspoon Yellow Chartreuse
- 1 dash Regan's Orange Bitters

Stir with ice and strain into a cocktail coupe. Garnish with a lemon twist.

Snare Drum

Drink's California Gold made this rum variation of the classic High Hat for a Banks Rum event.

- 2 oz Banks Rum
- 1/2 oz Cherry Heering
- 1/2 oz Lemon Juice
- 1/4 oz Orgeat
- 1/4 oz Cinnamon Syrup
- 1 dash Peychaud's Bitters

Shake with ice and strain into a cocktail glass. Twist a lemon peel over the top.

Soekarno

Matt Schrage at No. 9 Park based this drink off of the Petion cocktail from Haiti.

- 2 oz Old Monk Rum
- 1 oz Bénédictine
- 1/2 oz Batavia Arrack
- 1 oz Lime Juice

Shake with ice and strain into a cocktail glass.

Sous le Soleil

Created by Drink's California Gold for a Grand Marnier event held there in 2009.

- 1 1/2 oz Pierre Ferrand Cognac
- 3/4 oz Grand Marnier
- 1/4 oz Maraschino Liqueur
- 1/4 oz Cynar
- 1/4 oz Del Maguey Minero Mezcal
- 1 dash Fee's Whiskey Barrel Bitters

Stir with ice and strain into a rocks glass.

Spanish Caravan,
Island Creek
Oyster Bar

Spanish Caravan

One of the early drinks on the Island Creek Oyster Bar menu.

1 oz Daron Calvados
1 oz Herradura Reposado Tequila
3/4 oz Lustau East India Solera Sherry
1/4 oz St. Elizabeth Allspice Dram

Stir with ice and strain into a coupe glass. Optional: garnish with a spiced dehydrated apple slice.

Staghorn

Jane at Temple Bar in Cambridge riffed on the Corpse Reviver #2.

1 oz Tanqueray Gin
1 1/4 oz Cocchi Americano
3/4 oz Zirbenz Stone Pine Liqueur
3/4 oz Lemon Juice
2 dash Sambuca

Shake with ice and strain into a cocktail glass.

Starbird

An elegant beer cocktail by Sahil Mehta of Estragon who used the apple-fennel pairing as his muse.

❖ 3-4 oz oz Unibroue Éphémère Beer
❖ 1 oz St. Germain
❖ 1/6 Granny Smith Apple (cubed)

Muddle the apple cubes in St. Germain. Add 1 oz of beer and fine strain into a wine glass rinsed with Camargo Absinthe. Add 2-3 oz more beer and garnish with several drops of Angostura Bitters.

St. Argent

Created by Joy Richard at the Franklin Southie for a St. Germain industry night in 2009.

❖ 1 oz Milagro Silver Tequila
❖ 1 oz St. Germain
❖ 1 oz Campari

Stir with ice, strain into a cocktail glass, and garnish with an orange twist.

Start of a New Road

Sam Treadway at Backbar used Chris McMillian's End of the Road in Beta Cocktails as a starting point.

❖ 1/2 oz Lagavulin Scotch
❖ 1/2 oz Campari
❖ 1/2 oz Green Chartreuse
❖ 3/4 oz Neisson Rhum Agricole Blanc
❖ 3/4 oz Lime Juice

Shake with ice and strain into a coupe glass.

Storm Chaser

A coastal-inspired Flip at No. 9 Park.

❖ 1 oz Smith & Cross Rum
❖ 1 oz Carpano Sweet Vermouth
❖ 1 oz Cynar
❖ 1/2 oz Simple Syrup
❖ 1 Whole Egg
❖ 2 dash Bitter Science Fruitcake Bitters (sub Angostura)

Shake without ice and then with ice. Strain into a rocks glass.

ST

Straits of Messina

This Italian-themed sparkler was crafted at Island Creek Oyster Bar in Boston.

- 3 Green Cardamom Pods
- 1 pinch Salt
- 2 dash Regan's Orange Bitters
- 1 1/2 oz Cocchi Americano
- 3/4 oz Blood Orange Juice

Muddle cardamom, salt, and bitters. Add the rest of the ingredients and ice. Shake and double strain into a cocktail or wine glass. Top with ~2 oz of Dibon Cava.

Strange Bedfellows

Citizen's Sean Frederick's contribution to a J.D. Salinger-themed charity event held at the Hawthorne.

- 2 oz Glenlivet 12 Year Scotch
- 3/4 oz Cocchi Sweet Vermouth
- 1/2 oz Aperol
- 1 barspoon Maraschino Liqueur

Stir with ice and strain into a rocks glass rinsed Caol Ila Scotch and containing coffee ice cubes. Twist an orange peel over the top.

Strasbourg

A medley of European ingredients brought together by Sahil Mehta of Estragon.

- 1 oz Aalborg Aquavit
- 1 oz Hayman's Old Tom Gin
- 1 oz Noilly Prat Dry Vermouth
- 1 dash Rothman & Winter Crème de Violette

Stir with ice and strain into a cocktail coupe. Garnish with a lemon twist.

Strawberry Swizzle

Created at the Citizen Public House in Boston.

- 1 1/2 oz Lustau Amontillado Sherry
- 3/4 oz Green Chartreuse
- 3/4 oz Strawberry Syrup
- 1/2 oz Lime Juice

Build in a Collins glass filled with crushed ice and swizzle to mix. Garnish with a lime wedge and add a straw.

Streets of Gettysburg

Created by Misty Kalkofen at Brick and Mortar.

❖
❖
❖ 1 1/4 oz Lustau Dry Amontillado
❖ Sherry
❖ 1 oz Rittenhouse 100 Rye
❖ 1/2 oz Bénédictine
❖ 1/4 oz Galliano Ristretto Coffee
❖ Liqueur
❖ 1 dash Angostura Bitters
❖
❖ *Stir with ice and strain into a rocks*
❖ *glass. Twist an orange peel over the*
❖ *top.*
◆

Summer of Sureau

Misty Kalkofen came up with this drink at Green Street for the first St. Germain Can-Can Classic.

❖
❖ 1 1/2 oz St. Germain
❖ 1/2 oz Batavia Arrack
❖ 1/2 oz Lemon Juice
❖ 1/4 oz Pineapple Syrup
❖ 3 dash Bittermens Boston Bittahs
❖
❖ *Shake with ice and strain into a*
❖ *cocktail glass.*
❖
◆

Super Nova

Drink's John Gertsen was inspired by George Kappeler's Star Cocktail from 1895, and he took it to another level.

❖ 1 3/4 oz Laird's Bonded Apple
❖ Brandy
❖ 3/4 oz Carpano Sweet Vermouth
❖ 1/2 oz Simple Syrup
❖ 1 dash Fee's Whiskey Barrel
❖ Bitters
❖ 1 dash Angostura Bitters

❖ *Muddle 3 cardamom pods in the apple*
❖ *brandy. Add rest of ingredients and ice*
❖ *and stir. Add 1/4 oz Green Chartreuse*
❖ *to a rocks glass and ignite. Twist a*
❖ *lemon peel over the fire and drop in to*
❖ *carmelize. Douse the flame after 15*
❖ *seconds by double straining the chilled*
❖ *ingredients into the rocks glass.*
❖

Sun Rays Illu-minate Smoke Filled Haze

Aaron Butler at Russell House Tavern named his beer Highball after a Matisyahu song lyric.

- 1 1/2 oz Lillet Blanc
- 1 1/4 oz Laphroaig 10 Year Scotch
- 3/4 oz Averell Damson Plum Gin
- 3/4 oz Lemon Juice
- 3/4 oz Honey Syrup

Shake with ice and strain into a Highball glass filled with fresh ice. Top with 1-2 oz Victory Golden Monkey Beer Abbey Tripel and add a straw. Substitute sloe gin for the Averell.

Surbiton Road

Eastern Standard's Naomi Levi imagined what drinks they would make at the Italian Consulate in Kingston, Jamaica, using ingredients from both cultures.

- 1/2 Lime (cut into wedges)
- 12 Basil Leaves
- 1 oz Vanilla Syrup
- 1 oz Smith & Cross Rum
- 1/2 oz Cruzan Black Strap Rum
- 1/2 oz Punt e Mes

Muddle lime, basil, and syrup. Add rest of ingredients and ice, shake, and double strain into a rocks glass filled with crushed ice. Garnish with a basil sprig and add a straw.

Sureau Fizz

Ben Sandrof won the first St. Germain Can-Can Classic with this Ramos Gin Fizz variation.

- 2 oz Beefeater Gin
- 1 oz St. Germain
- 1/2 oz Lemon Juice
- 1/2 oz Lime Juice
- 1/2 oz Simple Syrup
- 1 1/2 oz Heavy Cream
- 1 Egg White
- 1 drop Orange Blossom Water

Shake without ice and then with ice. Strain into a Highball glass containing 2 oz of soda water. Twist an orange peel over the top, garnish with 3-4 additional drops of orange blossom water, and add a straw.

Swamp Water Fix,
No. 9 Park

Svanberg

*Fred Yarm riffed on the classic
Hoop La in this homage to a
Swedish surrealist artist.*

❖ 3/4 oz Gin
❖ 3/4 oz Lime Juice
❖ 3/4 oz Swedish Punsch
❖ 3/4 oz Curaçao

❖ *Shake with ice and strain into a
cocktail glass.*

Swamp Water Fix

*No. 9 Park's Ted Kilpatrick up-
dated the Swamp Water, a drink
served at the old Rathskeller in
Boston.*

❖ 1 1/2 oz Green Chartreuse
❖ 1 oz Batavia Arrack
❖ 1/2 oz Pineapple Syrup
❖ 1/2 oz Pineapple Juice
❖ 3/4 oz Lime Juice
❖ 2 drop Bitter Truth Celery Bitters

❖ *Build in a water goblet. Fill with
crushed ice and swizzle to mix. In-
sert a wide lime twist in the glass,
top with ice, and add a straw.*

151

Taggart Cocktail

When Eastern Standard's Amer Picon stock ran out, Nicole Lebedevitch made some substitutions to keep the spirit of Chuck's Hoskins Cocktail alive at the bar.

- 2 oz Beefeater Gin
- 1/2 oz Cynar
- 1/2 oz Clement Creole Shrub
- 1/4 oz Maraschino Liquour
- 1/4 oz Mirto

Stir with ice and strain into a chilled coupe. Garnish with a flamed lemon twist.

Tally-ho!

One of Eastern Standard's more popular offerings on the Pimm's section of their menu.

- 2 oz Pimm's No. 1
- 1/2 oz Grenadine
- 1/2 oz Lemon Juice
- 1 barspoon St. Elizabeth Allspice Dram
- 1 dash Bittermens Tiki Bitters

Shake with ice and strain into a cocktail glass.

Tanglin Club

Fred Yarm crossed the Pegu Club with the Scofflaw and named the drink after another 19th century club.

- 1 oz Gin
- 1 oz Dry Vermouth
- 1/2 oz Passion Fruit Syrup
- 1/2 oz Lime Juice
- 2 dash Angostura Bitters

Shake with ice and strain into a cocktail glass. Garnish with an orange twist.

Teardrop

Created by Misty Kalkofen at Brick and Mortar in Cambridge.

- 1 1/2 oz Cardamaro
- 1 oz Ransom Old Tom Gin
- 1/4 oz Averna
- 1/2 tsp Pernod Absinthe

Stir with ice and strain into a rocks glass.

Temporary Fix

Misty Kalkofen took a Mississippi Mule and converted it into a 19th century-style drink at Brick and Mortar in Cambridge.

2 oz Citadelle Gin
1/2 oz Crème de Cassis
3/4 oz Lemon Juice
1/4 oz Simple Syrup

Shake with ice and strain into a rocks glass filled with crushed ice. Garnish with a lemon twist and add straws.

Tequila Mockingbird

Created by Bryn Tattan at Drink in Boston.

2 oz Del Maguey Mezcal Vida
1/2 oz Lime Juice
1/2 oz Agave Nectar
1 Egg White

Shake without ice and then with ice. Strain into a rocks glass and garnish with 10 drops of Peychaud's Bitters.

Tequila Scaffa

Scott Holliday crafted this at Rendezvous for a bar patron who rather enjoyed Scott's Rum Scaffa.

2 oz Milagro Añejo Tequila
1 oz Maurin Quinquina

Build in a rocks glass without ice, stir briefly, and garnish with a lime twist. Note: this is a room-temperature drink.

The # Tres

Todd Maul of Clio in Boston based this cachaça drink off of the Corpse Reviver #2 but substituted grenadine for the absinthe.

3/4 oz Beija Cachaça
3/4 oz Lime Juice
3/4 oz Lillet Blanc
3/4 oz Luxardo Triple Sec

Shake with ice and strain into a coupe glass. Gently add a dash of grenadine so it sinks to the bottom.

Theresa No. 4

*Jackson Cannon at Eastern
Standard was inspired by the
Teresa from Gary Regan's The Joy
of Mixology.*

1 1/2 oz Crème de Cassis
3/4 oz London Dry Gin
3/4 oz Lime Juice
3/4 oz Campari

*Shake with ice and strain into a High-
ball glass filled with fresh ice. Top with
2-3 oz soda water, garnish with a mint
sprig, and add a straw.*

Thin Mint Julep

*An herbal and complex Julep
invented at Lineage in Brookline.*

2 oz Fernet Branca
1 oz Crème de Cacao

*Lightly muddle 2 sprigs of mint in
some of the crème de cacao. Add
crushed ice and the rest of the ingredients. Stir and top off with more
ice. Garnish with 2 sprigs of mint
and add a straw.*

This, That, the
Other,
The Independent

Third Street

Abigail's developed this tribute to their locale in Cambridge.

- 1 1/2 oz Gin
- 1 1/2 oz Lillet
- 1/2 oz Lustau Dry Amontillado Sherry
- 2 dash Regan's Orange Bitters

Stir with ice and strain into a cocktail glass. Garnish with a flamed orange twist.

This, That, the Other

An elegant tequila aperitif by Isaac Sussman at the Independent in Somerville.

- 2 oz Maurin Quina
- 1 oz Chinaco Blanco Tequila
- 1/2 oz Graham Six Grapes Port
- 1 dash Lime Bitters (such as Scrappy's)
- 1 dash Angostura Bitters

Stir with ice and strain into a coupe glass. Garnish with a lime twist.

Thompson Schneider

Citizen Public House's variation on the Half Sinner, Half Saint that Chad Arnholt named after two of his roommates, one of whom is Will Thompson of Drink.

- 1 1/2 oz Cocchi Americano
- 1 1/2 oz Cocchi Sweet Vermouth

Build on ice in a rocks glass and stir. Top with 1 oz of ginger beer and float 2 dashes of Kübler Absinthe on top. Add a straw.

Throw the Gun #2

John Mayer's tribute at Craigie on Main to the cinematic moment where a bandit is out of bullets so he drops the gun, turns, and runs.

- 1 oz Citadelle Reserve Gin
- 3/4 oz Dry Oloroso Sherry
- 3/4 oz Zucca
- 1/2 oz Simple Syrup
- 1/4 oz Lime Juice
- 1 dash Angostura Bitters
- 1 pinch Salt
- 1 Whole Egg

Shake without ice and then with ice. Strain into a coupe glass.

TI

Ticket to Paradise

Created at Worcester's Citizen Restaurant.

1 oz Milagro Silver Tequila
1 oz Plymouth Sloe Gin
1 oz Swedish Punsch
1 barspoon Lemon Juice
2 dash Fee's Rhubarb Bitters

Stir with ice and strain into a cocktail glass. Garnish with a lemon twist.

Tiki Ghosn

Influenced by the Jungle Bird, Fred Yarm's whiskey Tikism was named after an infamous cage fighter.

2 oz Bourbon
1/2 oz Crème de Cacao
1/2 oz Campari
1/2 oz Pineapple Juice
1/2 oz Lime Juice

Shake with ice and strain into a rocks glass or Tiki mug filled with crushed ice. Garnish with a dash or two of mole bitters and add a straw.

Ti' Punch Fizz

Drink's Ezra Star gave the classic Ti' Punch the Ramos Gin Fizz treatment.

2 oz La Favorite Rhum Agricole Blanc
1 oz Lime Juice
1 oz Simple Syrup
1 1/2 oz Cream
2 dash Bittermens Tiki Bitters
1 Egg White

Shake without ice and then with ice. Strain into a Highball glass containing 2 oz soda water. Add a straw and garnish with a lime twist.

Tobacconist

A smokey number created by California Gold at Drink in Boston.

1 1/2 oz Del Maguey Mezcal Vida
1/2 oz Galliano Ristretto Coffee Liqueur
1/2 oz Grapefruit Juice
1/2 oz Lemon Juice
1/4 oz Lustau Pedro Ximénez Sherry
1 barspoon St. Elizabeth Allspice Dram
1 dash Angostura Bitters
1 dash Fee's Whiskey Barrel Bitters

Shake with ice and strain into a goblet filled with crushed ice. Float 1/4 oz Del Maguey Chichicapa Mezcal and add straws.

Todd Cocktail

Todd Maul's tribute to David Embury and William Boothby at Clio.

2 oz Rittenhouse 100 Rye
1 oz Aperol
1 oz Dolin Sweet Vermouth
1 dash Angostura Bitters

Stir with ice and strain into a cocktail glass.

Tommy Noble

A B Side Lounge drink brought over to Deep Ellum by the drink's creator, Dave Cagle; it is named after a notoriously bad British Boxer in the early part of the 1900s.

1 1/4 oz Plymouth Gin
1 1/4 oz Pimm's No. 1
1/2 oz Lemon Juice
1/2 oz Simple Syrup
1 dash Aromatic Bitters

Shake with ice and strain into a cocktail glass. Garnish with an orange twist.

TO

Tom Terrific

Daren Swisher's tribute to the Patriot's Tom Brady created at Park Restaurant in Harvard Square.

❖ 1 3/4 oz Hayman's Old Tom Gin
❖ 1/2 oz Cherry Herring
❖ 1/2 oz Lemon Juice
❖ 1/2 oz Simple Syrup

Shake with ice and strain into a Collins glass containing ice cubes. Top with 2-3 oz Great Divide's Titan IPA, garnish with an orange slice and cherry, and add a straw.

Too Much, Too Little, Too Late

For Valentine's Day in 2012, Misty Kalkofen whipped up a short list of bitter drinks at Brick and Mortar including this one.

❖ 1 1/4 oz Tanqueray 10 Gin
❖ 1 oz Cocchi Americano
❖ 3/4 oz Gran Classico
❖ 1/4 oz Rothman & Winter Apricot Liqueur
❖ 2 dash Orange Bitters

Stir with ice and strain into a cocktail glass.

Tony Montana

A rum Preakness-like tribute to Al Pacino's character in Scarface at Trina's Starlite Lounge in Somerville.

❖ 2 oz Pyrat Rum
❖ 3/4 oz Carpano Sweet Vermouth
❖ 1 barspoon Bénédictine
❖ 3 dash Orange Bitters

Stir with ice and strain into a cocktail glass. Garnish with a cherry and an orange twist.

Torontino

The result of a Toronto crossed with a Milano-Torino (a/k/a an Americano) at J.M. Curley.

❖ 1 1/2 oz Forty Creek Canadian Whisky
❖ 1/2 oz Fernet Branca
❖ 1/2 oz Campari
❖ 1/2 oz Dubonnet Rouge

Stir with ice and strain into a cocktail coupe. Twist a lemon peel over the top.

Trenton

This ode to New Jersey was crafted at Deep Ellum in Allston.

❖ 1 3/4 oz Laird's Applejack
❖ 1/2 oz Cinnamon Syrup
❖ 1/2 oz Cardamaro
❖ 1/4 Cinzano Sweet Vermouth
❖ 2 dash Herbsaint
❖ 2 dash Angostura Bitters
❖ 2 dash Peychaud's Bitters
❖

❖ *Stir with ice and strain into a rocks*
❖ *glass. Twist an orange peel over the*
◆ *top.*

Tres Pinas

Estragon's Sahil Mehta thematic hat trick of agave, pineapple, and artichoke.

❖ 1 1/2 oz Del Maguey Crema de
❖ Mezcal
❖ 1/2 oz Small Hand Foods
❖ Pineapple Gum Syrup
❖ 1/2 oz Lime Juice
❖ 1/4 oz Cynar

❖ *Shake with ice and strain into a*
❖ *cocktail coupe glass. Substitute*
❖ *1 1/2 oz regular mezcal plus 1 tsp*
   agave nectar for the Crema.

Tom Terrific,
Park Restaurant

TW-UN

Two From L.A.

A complex herbal drink from Clio.

- 2 oz Cynar
- 1 oz No. 3 London Dry Gin
- 1/2 oz Green Chartreuse
- 2 dash Orange Bitters
- 1 Egg White

Shake without ice and then with ice. Strain into a rocks glass and garnish with an orange twist.

Two Worlds Sour

One of Ben Sandrof's creations for his Sunday Salon speakeasy series.

- 1 oz Neisson Rhum Agricole Blanc
- 1 oz Balvenie Doublewood Scotch
- 1/2 oz Lapsang Souchong Tea Syrup
- 1/2 oz Lemon Juice
- 1 dash Angostura Bitters

Shake with ice and strain into a cocktail glass. Twist a lemon peel over the top.

Union Cocktail

Brother Cleve represented the cultural history of Union Square for the Somerville Arts Council, and the drink later appeared on the Independent's menu.

- 2 oz Michael Collins Irish Whiskey
- 1 oz Blandy's Rainwater Madeira
- 1/2 oz Meletti Amaro
- 1 dash Regan's Orange Bitters
- 1 dash Angostura Bitters

Stir with ice and strain into a cocktail coupe. Garnish with an orange twist.

Union Derby

Backbar's adaptation of the Brown Derby that they named after their neighborhood.

- 1 1/2 oz Four Roses Bourbon
- 3/4 oz Drambuie 15 Year
- 3/4 oz Pink Grapefruit Juice
- 1 dash Peychaud's Bitters

Shake with ice and strain into a coupe glass.

Union Station Swizzle

Drink's California Gold developed this Swizzle to serve at her guest shift at the Patterson House in Nashville.

❖
❖ 2 oz Eagle Rare Bourbon
❖ 1/2 oz Maraschino Liqueur
❖ 1/2 oz Apricot Liqueur
❖ 1/2 oz Lemon Juice
❖
❖ *Add to a Highball glass filled with*
❖ *crushed ice. Swizzle to mix, float a*
❖ *dash of Herbsaint and 3 dashes of*
❖ *Angostura Bitters on top, and add a*
❖ *straw.*

Valkyrie

Sam Gabrielli at Temple Bar was inspired by Evan Harrison's Peralta.

❖ 2 oz Rittenhouse 100 Rye
❖ 1/2 oz Averna
❖ 1/2 oz Cynar
❖ 1/4 oz St. Germain
❖
❖ *Stir with ice and strain into a rocks*
❖ *glass. Twist a grapefruit peel over*
❖ *the top.*

Velvet Goldmine

Evan Kenney's glam rock tribute at Temple Bar in Cambridge.

❖ 2 oz Del Maguey Mezcal Vida
❖ 1/2 oz Velvet Falernum
❖ 1/2 oz Fernet Branca
❖ 1/2 oz Pineapple Juice
❖ 3/4 oz Lime Juice
❖ 1/4 oz Agave Nectar
❖ 1 dash Peychaud's Bitters
❖
❖ *Shake with ice and strain into a*
❖ *rocks glass filled with crushed ice.*
❖ *Garnish with a mint sprig and add*
❖ *straws.*

Vida Rebellion

Joy Richard's mezcal riff on the Negroni at the Citizen Public House in Boston.

❖ 1 oz Del Maguey Mezcal Vida
❖ 1 oz Lustau Dry Oloroso Sherry
❖ 1 oz Gran Classico
❖ 2 dash Angostura Orange Bitters
❖
❖ *Stir with ice and strain into a cock-*
❖ *tail glass. Garnish with an orange*
❖ *twist.*

᚛᚛᚛᚛᚛᚛᚛᚛᚛᚛᚛᚛᚛᚛᚛᚛᚛᚛

West Fens,
Citizen Public House

Vincelli Fizz

Eastern Standard's Jackson Cannon became a finalist for Bénédictine's "Alchemists of Our Age" contest in 2010 with this Fizz.

❖ 1 1/2 oz Bénédictine
❖ 1 1/2 oz Rosé Vermouth
❖ 1/2 oz Lemon Juice
❖ 1 Egg White

❖ *Shake without ice and then with ice. Strain into a coupe glass and top with 1 oz of dry sparkling wine. Optional: garnish with a few spritzes of flamed madjool date infusion.*

Vincent Rose

Ryan Lotz crafted this blueberry thrill at Lineage.

❖ 3/4 oz Anchor Genevieve Gin
❖ 3/4 oz Averna
❖ 3/4 oz Maraschino Liqueur
❖ 3/4 oz Lemon Juice
❖ 1 heaping barspoon Blueberry Jam (~3/16 oz)

❖ *Shake with ice and double strain into a cocktail glass.*

Ward 8

The Ward 8 is an old school Boston drink created at the Locke-Ober Restaurant cerca 1898. This is an adaptation of how Drink in Boston stylishly presents the classic.

❖ 3/4 oz Lemon Juice
❖ 3/4 oz Orange Juice
❖ 1 barspoon Sugar
❖ 2 oz Rye Whiskey
❖ 3/8-1/2 oz Grenadine

❖ *Stir juices with sugar until the crystals dissolves. Add rye, shake with ice, and strain into a red wine glass that had its insides rubbed with a mint sprig. Fill with crushed ice, and drizzle the grenadine over the top so it will cascade down to the bottom of the glass. Garnish with a fresh mint sprig and an orange peel spiral twist, and add a straw.*

◆

Wayback

Created by Max Toste at Deep Ellum in Allston.

❖ 1 1/2 oz Fidencio Mezcal
❖ 1/2 oz Cocchi Barolo Chinato
❖ 1/2 oz Carpano Sweet Vermouth
❖ 1/4 oz Amer Picon (or Picon replica)
❖ 1/4 oz Agave Nectar
❖ 2 dash Angostura Bitters

❖ *Stir with ice and strain into a cocktail coupe. Twist a lemon peel and an orange peel over the top.*

◆

West Fens

Sean Frederick crafted a Manhattan-like tribute to the Citizen Public House's neighborhood.

❖ 1 1/2 oz Tuthilltown's Hudson Manhattan Rye
❖ 3/4 oz Aperol
❖ 1/2 oz Carpano Sweet Vermouth
❖ 1/4 oz Maraschino Liqueur
❖ 2 dash Jerry Thomas Decanter Bitters

❖ *Stir with ice and strain into a coupe glass. Serve with a brandied cherry.*

Wheelwright

An aperitif created by West Bridge's Josh Taylor in honor of the nearby bridge's architect. Soon after, the drink helped him win a Golden Vespa in a Galliano Contest.

1 1/2 oz Tio Pepe Palomino Fino Sherry
1 oz Dolin Blanc Vermouth
3/4 oz Galliano
1/2 oz Wray & Nephew White Overproof Rum

Stir with ice and strain into a cocktail glass. Garnish with 2 drops orange blossom water.

Whiskey_A_ Go_Go

Scott Holliday at Rendezvous was inspired by the return of the old Galliano formulation.

1 1/4 oz Bourbon
1 oz Pineapple Juice
1/2 oz Galliano
1/4 oz Lemon Juice
1/4 oz Simple Syrup

Shake with ice and strain into a cocktail glass. Top off with ~2 oz prosecco.

White Devil

Allston's Deep Ellum tinkered with a Rum Martini called the Black Devil that appears in the Playboy's Host & Bar Book.

3/4 oz El Dorado 3 Year White Rum
3/4 oz Cocchi Americano
3/4 oz Dolin Blanc Vermouth
3/4 oz Maraschino Liqueur
2 dash Orange Bitters

Stir with ice and strain into a coupe glass. Garnish with a Marasca cherry.

White Lie

Based off the Cuban exile declaration that there is no free Cuba under Castro, Ted Kilpatrick created this riff on the Cuba Libre at No. 9 Park.

1 oz Wray & Nephew Overproof White Rum
3/4 oz Old Monk Rum
1/2 oz Angostura Bitters

Stir with ice and strain into a rocks glass rinsed with Herbsaint. Top with 2 oz Coca Cola.

White Hook

Ryan Lotz was inspired by Deep Ellum's White Manhattan and concocted this Red Hook variation at Lineage.

❖ 2 oz Bols Genever
❖ 1/2 oz Vya Dry Vermouth
❖ 1/2 oz Maraschino Liqueur
❖ 1 dash Regan's Orange Bitters

Stir with ice and strain into a rocks glass. Garnish with a lemon twist.

White Manhattan

Deep Ellum's Max Toste modified a Genever take on the Manhattan by crossing it with an Old Fashioned.

❖ 2 oz Bols Genever
❖ 1 oz Dolin Blanc Vermouth
❖ 1 Sugar Cube
❖ 2 dash Wormwood Bitters (such as Cocktail Kingdom's)

Dash bitters onto a sugar cube and muddle. Add rest of ingredients and ice, stir, and strain into a rocks glass. Garnish with a lemon twist.

WiFi

This riff on the Marconi Wireless was created by Drink's Josey Packard for a James Beard Awards event in 2009.

❖ 1 3/4 oz Laird's Bonded Apple Brandy
❖ 1 oz Lillet Blanc
❖ 1/4 oz Drambuie
❖ 1/8 oz Honey Syrup
❖ 2 dash Peychaud's Bitters

Stir with ice and strain into a cocktail glass.

Wildwood

Bobby McCoy developed this drink for the rehearsal dinner before his wedding, and he later put it on the Island Creek Oyster Bar menu.

❖ 2 oz Rittenhouse 100 Rye
❖ 1/2 oz Cinnamon Syrup
❖ 1/2 oz Amaro Nonino
❖ 2 dash Angostura Bitters
❖ 2 dash Peychaud's Bitters
❖ 6 drop Pernod Absinthe

Stir with ice and strain into a rocks glass. Garnish with an orange twist.

Wilhelm Scream

A tribute to an infamous movie sound effect crafted by John Mayer at Craigie on Main.

- 1 1/2 oz Del Maguey Mezcal Vida
- 1/2 oz La Favorite Amber Rhum Agricole
- 1/2 oz Caol Ila 10 Year Scotch
- 1/2 oz Yellow Chartreuse
- 1 squeeze Lemon Peel

Stir with ice and strain into a rocks glass with a large ice cube. Twist another piece of lemon peel over the top and discard.

William of Orange

Emily Stanley then of Green Street presented this drink for the Bartenders on the Rise event in 2010.

- 1 1/2 oz Bols Genever
- 1/2 oz Bénédictine
- 1/2 oz Punt e Mes
- 1/2 oz Aperol
- 2 dash Orange Bitters

Stir with ice and strain into a rocks glass. Twist an orange peel over the top.

Wing Nang

The Maurin's almond notes donate a rather Tiki feel to the Independent's drink.

- 1 oz Old Monk Rum
- 1 oz Palo Viejo White Rum
- 3/4 oz Maurin Quina
- 1 1/4 oz Grapefruit Juice
- 1/2 oz Cinnamon Syrup
- 4 dash Bittermens Tiki Bitters

Shake with ice and pour into a rocks glass. Add straws.

Word to Your Mom

A Last Word variation created at Trina's Starlite Lounge in Somerville.

- 1/2 oz Bols Genever
- 1/2 oz Yellow Chartreuse
- 1/2 oz Maraschino Liqueur
- 1/2 oz Lemon Juice

Shake with ice and pour into a rocks glass. Top with 1 1/2 oz Pretty Things Jack D'Or Saison-style beer, garnish with a cherry, and add straws.

Word to
Your Mom,
Trina's Starlite
Lounge

Wong's Grog

*Randy Wong made this variation
of the classic Navy Grog at Clio.*

❖ 3/4 oz El Dorado 5 Year Rum
❖ 3/4 oz Goslings Black Seal Rum
❖ 3/4 oz Rittenhouse 100 Rye
❖ 1/2 oz Lime Juice
❖ 1/2 oz Grapefruit Juice
❖ 1/2 oz Cinnamon Syrup
❖ 1/4 tsp Ground Kona Coffee Beans
❖ 1/4 tsp Vanilla Paste (sub Vanilla
❖   Extract)

*Infuse rums and rye with coffee in a
mixing glass for 5 minutes. Add rest
of ingredients and ice, shake, and
double strain into a rocks glass. The
glass can have an ice cone with a
lime wheel garnish or can be filled
with crushed ice with a lime twist
garnish.*

Yellow Jacket

This floral and herbal sparkler was developed at the Beehive in Boston.

- 1 oz Yellow Chartreuse
- 1 oz St. Germain
- 1/2 oz Lemon Juice

Shake with ice and strain into a Champagne flute. Top off with ~2 oz Mumm Napa sparkling wine and garnish with a lemon twist.

Zeeland

Created by Andrea Desrosiers and Fred Yarm for a Bols Genever industry event at the Franklin Southie.

- 1 1/2 oz Bols Genever
- 1/2 oz Lillet Blanc
- 1/2 oz Rothman & Winter Apricot Liqueur
- 1/2 oz Lime Juice
- 1 dash Orange Bitters

Shake with ice and strain into a cocktail glass.

Zelda Fitzgerald

Carrie Cole at Craigie on Main based this off of the bar's Camino Cocktail.

- 1 1/2 oz Rittenhouse 100 Rye
- 1/2 oz Cynar
- 1/2 oz Aperol
- 1/2 oz Mirto Liqueur
- 2 dash Angostura Bitters
- 2 dash Angostura Orange Bitters

Stir with ice and strain into a rocks glass. Garnish with a flamed lemon twist.

Zimmermann Telegram

Inspired by the 1917 diplomatic proposal from Germany to Mexico, No. 9 Park's Ted Kilpatrick created this hoppy Silver Fizz.

- 1 1/2 oz Milagro Blanco Tequila
- 1 oz Del Maguey Mezcal Vida
- 1 oz Lemon Juice
- 1 oz Simple Syrup
- 1/8 oz Kübler Absinthe
- 1 Egg White

Shake without ice and then with ice. Strain into a Highball glass and top with 2 oz Houblon Chouffe Dobbelen IPA Tripel beer.

Zocalo

Misty Kalkofen created this at Drink in Boston and named it after the parade grounds in Mexican cities.

2 oz Del Maguey Mezcal Vida
1/2 oz Canela Cinnamon Syrup
1/2 oz Dolin Dry Vermouth
2 dash Angostura Orange Bitters

Stir with ice and strain into a punch cup or cocktail glass. Twist a lemon peel over the top.

Zimmermann Telegram, No. 9 Park

Syrups

Syrups play important roles in cocktails. All syrups have a sweet component that can be useful to balance bitter, acidic, or alcohol heat elements in the drink. Often they are infused with fruit or spice, thus donating flavor to the cocktail. But the character of the sweetener itself can also provide an intriguing taste component, such as with darker sugars or honey.

One bonus of the cocktail renaissance is the bounty of syrup producers that have sprouted up in the marketplace. At the end of this section is a list of companies that produce syrups, and I note which of their syrups are relevant to the recipes in this book. Most bars exercise discretion on which syrups they will make and which they will buy, and likewise, the home bartender should too. I personally make most of my own syrups, but some are just easier to buy in my opinion, such as orgeat and passion fruit syrup.

In addition, there are several syrups in the collection, such as tea, honey ginger, and certain spiced syrups, that are not ready-made commercially. However, most of these are easy to make with a little kitchen know-how. For kitchen tools, I recommend a covered pot, spoon for stirring, timer, funnel, mesh strainer, tea towel, and bottles. In terms of containers, I have used a wide assortment of plastic and glass bottles, both screw-top and swing-top, as well as Tupperware-like containers on occasion. While all of the syrups can be made on the stove, some simple ones can be made quickly in the microwave. The microwave is helpful for making small volumes of syrups in coffee mugs – just be careful not to let them boil over which can happen when running the microwave in long bursts.

For some easy-to-make syrups like tea ones, I recommend making them in small volumes each time. But certain syrups, such as simple syrup and grenadine, are used more heavily and preserve well in the refrigerator. One trick for preserving syrups is to add alcohol to prevent microbial growth; note that this is not recommended if you also serve teetotalers who are abstaining from any and all alcohol. I recommend one ounce of 80-proof vodka for every 12 to 15 ounces of syrup; this is enough proof to stop most bacteria and some fungi. Instead of spiking the spirit in at the end, I add the vodka to the bottle, seal it, and shake it around to sterilize the inside of the bottle and cap. Leave the vodka in the bottle and add the syrup on top of it; seal the bottle and upend it a few times to mix.

Having lost a pricy bottle of B.G. Reynolds syrup to the "fuzzies," I also recommend adding the same proportion of alcohol to store-bought syrups to keep them from growing mold or bacteria. The amount of alcohol I recommend is not enough to stop all microbial growth, though. To minimize the risks of microbes getting in the bottle and to retard their growth, I recommend reducing the amount of time the cap is off the bottle, as well as storing all syrups in the refrigerator.

For some of the berry syrups, there are ways to make the syrup quickly by muddling fruit with simple syrup. After a fine-straining step, the flavor and intensity can be matched on the spot without needing a proper home-made or store-bought syrup.

Finally, one of the more curious syrups in this collection is honey syrup. While the flavored honey syrups included on the list are understandable, why make a diluted honey syrup instead of using full-strength honey? Undiluted honey can be used if stirred into the drink before ice is added. However, once ice is added, undiluted honey will harden and be resistant to incorporation into the drink. Diluted honey syrup avoids this problem.

Syrup Recipes

Simple Syrup

> 1 cup Sugar
> 1 cup Water
>
> Heat and stir until the sugar has dissolved.
> Let cool.

Note: All syrups here are presented as 1:1 simple syrups and no rich 2:1 syrups are used. Also, a few recipes call for darker sugar syrups such as dark moscavado. A good middle ground sugar for syrups is demerara sugar or dehydrated sugar cane juice, although common white sugar will work well for most drinks.

Grenadine

>1 cup Pomegranate Juice
>1 cup Sugar

>Heat and stir until the sugar has dissolved. Let cool. Places like Eastern Standard add some orange flower water to their grenadine, so add a few dashes if desired.

Used in the Belle de Jour, Coup d'État, Door 74, Helen the Pacific, Maroquet Swizzle, Pink Poodle, Rome is Burning, Tally-ho!, The # Tres, and Ward 8.

Honey Syrup

>1/2 cup Honey
>1/2 cup Water

>Boil the water and add to the honey. Stir until the honey is integrated.

Note: not all honey syrups are 1:1; some are stronger, but this is one of the most common ratios.
Used in the 3185, Assembly Cocktail, Battle of Trafalgar, Bee Sting, Chappaquiddick, Czech Julep, Dancing Scotsman, Daisy Black, Fears and Failures, Fécamp 500, Frolic Fizz, Healer, Honey Bearer, Honey Fitz, Metamorphosis, Mexican Love Affair, Old Trousers, Posta Aerea, Roxbury Russet, Sacrilege, Sun Rays Illuminated Smoke Filled Haze, and WiFi.

Brown Sugar Syrup

>1 cup Dark Brown Sugar
>1 cup Water

>Heat and stir until the brown sugar has dissolved. Let cool.

Used in the Jerez Flip and Battle Royal Fizz.

Spiced Brown Sugar Syrup

1 cup Dark Brown Sugar
1 cup Water
1 Star Anise Pod
2 Allspice Berries

Bring to a boil and simmer for 5 minutes.
Let cool and strain. Recipe from Green
Street.

Used in the Ewing No. 33, Skipper's Flip, and Skipper's Punch.

Maple Sugar Syrup

1/2 cup Maple Sugar
1/2 cup Water

Heat and stir until the maple sugar has dissolved and let cool.

Note: This is different from maple syrup due to the tree sap being processed into a solid sugar. The resultant sugar syrup has the aroma of maple syrup but not the viscosity.
Used in the Magic Wand Malfunction.

Mint Syrup

1 cup White Sugar
1 cup Boiling Water
Leaves from 12 or more sprigs of Mint

Stir sugar into boiling water until dissolved. Add mint leaves and muddle. Allow mint leaves to steep an hour or more, up to overnight. Strain the leaves from syrup and discard. In a pinch, muddling the leaves of a mint sprig in 1 oz of simple syrup will work.

Used in the Native Rose, New Sensation, and No. 9 Palmyra.

Lavender Syrup

1/2 cup Water
1/2 cup Sugar
4 Tbsp Lavender

Heat until the sugar is dissolved. Let cool and fine strain. Recipe from Misty Kalkofen.

Used in the 1820.

Spiced Syrup

1 cup Water
1 cup Sugar
12 Cloves
1-2 Star Anise
1/8 tsp Ground Cinnamon

Bring water and spices to a gentle boil and then simmer for 2 minutes. Add sugar, stir to dissolve, and simmer 2 minutes more. Let cool and then fine strain. Recipe is from Eastern Standard.

Used in the Jimmy Lane Swizzle, Kyselý, Mount Orohena, and Mr. Monahan's Flip.

Tea Syrup

1 cup Water
1 cup Sugar
1 Tbsp Tea (or use 2 tea bags)

Boil water and steep the tea leaves for 5 minutes. Strain out the tea leaves (or remove tea bags) and stir in the sugar until dissolved.

- *Earl Grey for the Barbados Fix.*
- *Green for the Kobayashi Maru and Pokey Crocus.*
- *Lapsang Souchong for the Potaro Punch and Two Worlds Sour.*
- *Rooibos for the Andora, Caledonian, and Flip Royal.*
- *Wu Wei for the Flapper Jane.*

Five Spice Syrup

1 cup Water
1 cup Sugar
1 Tbsp Five Spice Powder

Bring to a boil and simmer for 15 minutes.
Let cool and strain.

Used in the Figawi and Joe's Fashion.

Cinnamon Syrup

1 cup Water
1 cup Sugar
3 Cinnamon Sticks

Crush the cinnamon sticks into small
pieces. Add water and sugar and bring to a
boil. Let simmer for 5 minutes. Let cool and
steep for an hour, and then strain.

*Used in the Angry Barista, Applewood, Bentiki Fizz,
Bourbon Derby Flip, Cinnamon Collins, Cuban Anole,
Dwight Street Book Club, Indian Summer Julep, J.R.T.,
Leonora Banks, Peniques, Penny Reel, Rapa Nui, Scarlet
Swizzle, Trenton, Wildwood, Wing Nang, Wong's Grog,
and Zócalo.*

Ginger Syrup

1 cup Water
1 cup Sugar
2 oz Ginger, approx. 2 inches (peeled and
sliced)

Heat sugar and water until dissolved. Add
ginger and bring to a boil. Let simmer for
10 minutes, cool and steep for at least 30
minutes, and then strain.

*Used in the Boston Bog, Jamaican Bobsled, Midnight
Elixir, Naughty Nanny, and Roots of Rum.*

Ginger Honey Syrup

1/2 cup Honey
1/2 cup Water
1 oz Ginger, approx. 1 inch (peeled and sliced)

Heat honey and water and stir to dissolve the honey. Add ginger and bring to a boil. Let simmer for 10 minutes, cool and steep for at least 30 minutes, and then strain.

Used in the Panacea and São Paulo Summer.

Pineapple Syrup

1 small Pineapple (peeled and cubed)
Just enough simple syrup to cover the pineapple cubes

Place pineapple cubes in a bowl. Add enough simple syrup to cover all the pineapple, and let the syrup infuse in a covered bowl for 24 hours. Strain syrup away from pineapple cubes. Squeezing some of the cubes to add some pineapple juice is recommended by some.

Used in the Bourbon Rumba, Hornet's Nest, Loose Translation, Maikai Mule, Pineapple Tree, Summer of Sureau, Swamp Water Fix, and Tres Piñas.

Passion Fruit Syrup

1 cup Frozen Passion Fruit Pulp (thawed)
1 cup Simple Syrup (see recipe above)

Beach Bum Berry's recipe is to mix these. Perhaps making it like pineapple syrup and straining would work too, but I have not tried either of these for I buy my passion fruit syrup from B.G. Reynolds.

Used in the Barbados Fix, Golden Monarch, and Tanglin Club.

Cucumber Syrup

1/4 cup Cucumber Juice (*)
1/4 cup Sugar

Stir juice with sugar until it is dissolved.
(*) Muddle cucumber chunks well and use
a fine mesh strainer.

*Used in the Down at the Dinghy. The juice itself is used
in the Irma la Douce.*

Berry Syrup

1 cup Blackberries or sliced Strawberries
1 cup Water
1 cup Sugar

Bring the ingredients to a boil and simmer
for 10 minutes. Mashing the berries slightly
with a spoon during this process would not
hurt. Strain when cooled.

In berry syrups, I have found that frozen
fruit works just as well as store-bought
fresh. During the growing season, fresh is
often cheaper, while during the off season,
frozen is the more affordable option. Moreover, in a pinch, muddling fruit in simple
syrup and fine straining will work well too.

• *Blackberry for the Ho Tally and Pride of the Neighborhood.*
• *Strawberry for the Cantante Para Mi Vida and Strawberry Swizzle.*

Vanilla Syrup

1 cup Water
1 cup Sugar
1 Vanilla Bean split lengthwise

Bring to a boil while stirring to dissolve
sugar. Let simmer for 5 minutes and cool
for 1 hour. Remove the vanilla bean.

Used in the Mad Monk Fizz and Surbiton Road.

Guinness Syrup

12 oz Guinness Stout
1 cup Sugar

Heat the beer to reduce to 8 oz (1 cup). Add
sugar, stir until dissolved, and let cool. In a
pinch, stirring equal parts of beer and
sugar until the sugar is dissolved will work.
Recipe from Misty Kalkofen.
Used in the Dark Horse.

Commercial Sources for Syrups

While I recommend making many of these syrups yourself, there are com-
mercial options out there. Some I actually recommend buying instead of
making unless you do not mind hunting out ingredients or spending a bit
of time in the kitchen. Below are some syrup manufacturers with high
marks going to B.G. Reynolds, Small Hands Foods, and Ginger People. Note
that these companies make other syrups that are not used in this book
and thus not listed here.

B.G. Reynolds

cinnamon syrup, falernum, ginger syrup, hibiscus grenadine, orgeat, passion fruit syrup, and vanilla syrup

Small Hands Foods

gomme simple syrup, orgeat, pineapple gum syrup, raspberry gum syrup, and grenadine

Ginger People

organic ginger syrup

Stirrings

simple syrup and grenadine

Fee Brothers

blackberry syrup, raspberry syrup, strawberry syrup, pineapple syrup, passion fruit syrup, cinnamon syrup, falernum, orgeat, and grenadine

Monin

pure cane simple syrup, raspberry syrup, strawberry syrup, blackberry syrup, pineapple syrup, vanilla syrup, cinnamon syrup, cucumber syrup, ginger syrup, mint syrup, lavender syrup, passion fruit syrup, almond syrup (orgeat), blackberry syrup, grenadine

Torani

almond syrup (orgeat), blackberry syrup, strawberry syrup, raspberry syrup, cinnamon syrup, ginger syrup, passion fruit syrup, pineapple syrup, and vanilla syrup

Index of Drinks by Where Created (and Sometimes Where Served)

CPSIA information can be obtained at www.ICGtesting.com
Printed in the USA
BVOW03s1107231114

376355BV00009B/89/P